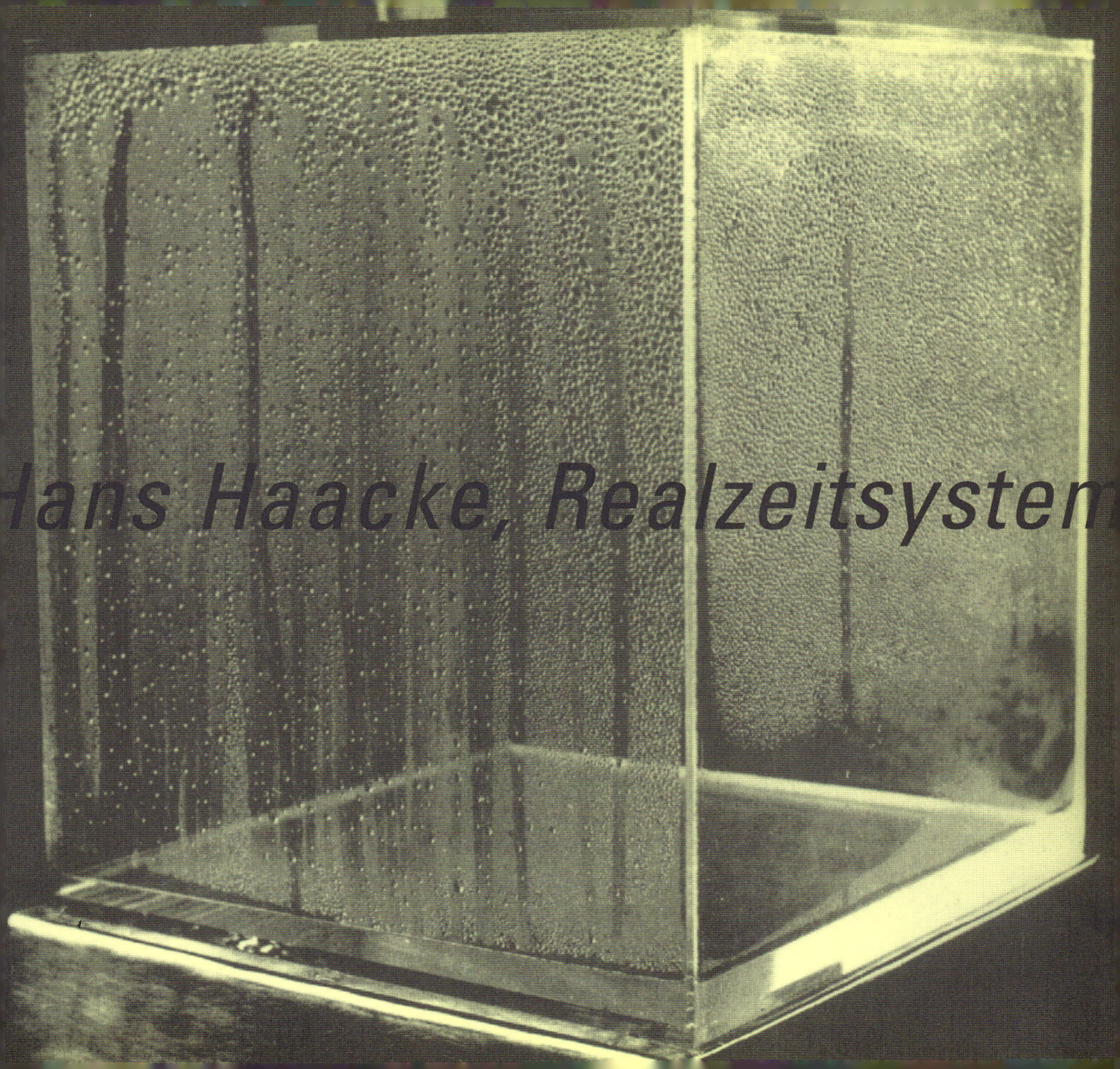

Hans Haacke, Realzeitsystem

Architecture is an interface. Not just now: it always has been.

The history of architecture is the history of the development of that interface between reality, architects, and the users of their architectures. Until now the architect has been the only source of production of form. His labor is hardly interactive with other elements or with reality itself. The information put out by architecture moves just one way.

INFORMATION

In our own era the quantity of information travelling around the world is steadily increasing, and all the media are 'feeding' off this. The handling of information has become the standard way of organizing reality. Subsequently each discipline physically develops its own particular procedures. Industries, economies, the means of production as a whole. Architecture too.

A mere operative change, it seems, yet it's more than that.

IN-FORM-ATION

The handling of information has, in part, a direct connection with form. Form is not only dependent on the subjectivity of a given author, but also on the handling of information about reality. A part of the 'unexpressible' aspect of architecture has come down on the side of its statistical treatment.

In a way architecture is not an art. It is, in fact, an anti-art. The artist takes the phenomena of reality and abstracts them from their context through his work. His production is the decontextualization of the art object, its 'removal from the circulation' of reality.

The architect, on the other hand, does exactly the opposite. He argues from the non-reality (of his ideas, that is), and sets this within the context of reality via his architectural work. His work is the contextualization, the 'putting into circulation' within reality of an architectural system.

The information era is also the era of interaction. If architecture can 'take' a form, it is possible to deduce that the architectural interface can be increasingly open, increasingly interactive. The architectural message no longer flows one way. It is no longer a closed system defined by the decision of the author, centered in the object, but an open system having to do with an undefined and incomplete procedure. Given this, the production of architecture does not attain a different state, but completely changes nature.

Thus, in architecture's physical scale - in which it may still be considered valid that energy is neither created nor destroyed - it may be concluded that, like energy, information alone is transformed. From reality to the construction process. And from the construction process onwards...

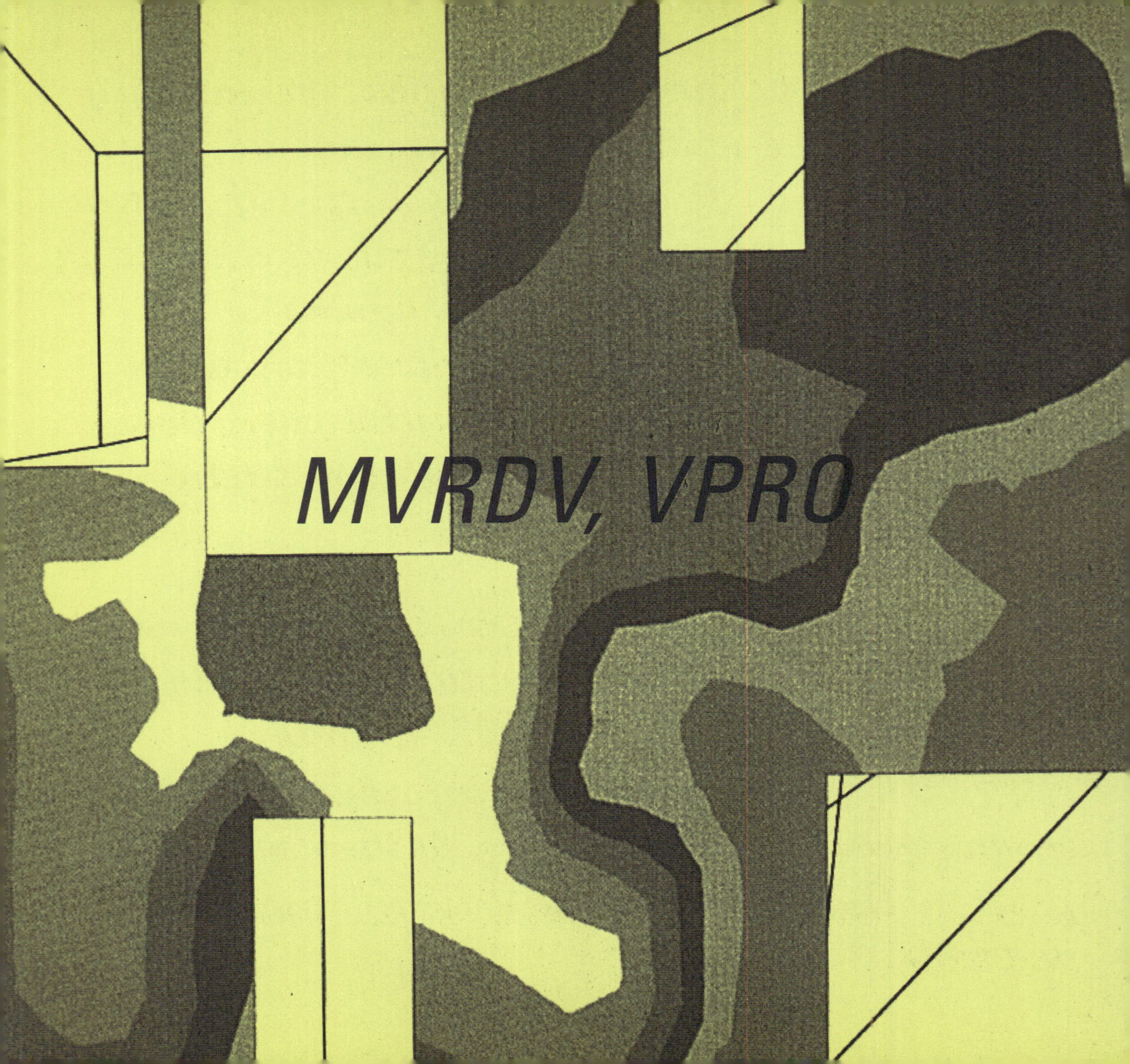
MVRDV, VPRO

Although it may not appear so, this book is based on a story more than on an architecture. The story of an architecture made for a producer of messages, a number of television and radio studios. An architecture which already has an informational goal per se; that is, for understanding and seeking, in reality itself, the generative bases of architectural form. A curious coincidence. The architects with the greatest experimental ambition in the architecture of the information era are commissioned to create the new headquarters of a media company whose rationale is also the unbiased exploration of reality. Therein lies the basis of the story.

And so this book sets out to consider architecture, once again, as the terrain of a more general argument about reality, and not merely the fact of producing buildings. A single 'science of creating architecture' does not exist, one that might be delimited or defined, just as the method through which it is manifested cannot be delimited. In this book, the book in itself, television, radio or architecture are not different media, but rather different messages springing from a single global medium of information. Thus, the story this book tells is the particular story of various 'generators of information' — VPRO — which, linking up with various 'generators of space' — MVRDV —, produce the result featured in these pages.

The epoch in which we live has increasingly adopted the motive power of information, to the point of converting this into the raw material, of sorts, of contemporary reality. We depend to such an extent on ways of handling information, whatever these may be, that no current procedure can now be understood without their presence. They have completely transformed our culture, our values and attitudes towards the world. The idea behind this book is that we take on board the idea that *in our own times the handling of information is becoming a basic code for acquiring knowledge about reality.*

This handling of information is to all intents and purposes transforming our way of understanding and applying any production process. And architecture, of course, is one of these processes.

We know that the computer era has now taken over once and for all.

The era of mechanization is passing away, but for all that only rarely do we assimilate, in concrete terms, the absolute transformation this entails.

Assimilating phenomena that still don't have a fixed structure to be assimilated is confusing. We find ourselves caught in a moment in which we have a clear notion of something being different, yet we persist in trying to understand this according to concepts that don't, on the whole, apply. In order to respond to certain things we'd do better to pose the right questions first.

Considering that architecture is to a large degree computerizable is not a mere formal or stylistic change. In fact it is not even a change. It is a global transformation of the medium, one which generates a different way of understanding processes. It is neither good nor bad. It is simply unstoppable. It is implanted in us, even though it is still difficult at times to assimilate it. *It is a process of 'secondary abstraction' – a computer abstraction on top of modern abstraction – which defines a different architecture,* as modern abstraction was also due to a transformation – an unstoppable one – of the method by which classical architecture was still being produced. To consider this transformation does not in the least imply, as could be argued, defending the definitive dehumanization of architecture, the overall delineation of procedures, the final dissolution of the artistic meaning implicit in architecture. Not at all. The opposite, in fact.

The computer abstraction of architecture transforms our way of understanding the production process, but also the very meaning of architecture as a productive activity in relation to reality.

Architecture as interface

If there is something the entire debate around architecture might agree on today it is the enormous complexity of the phenomena of reality in which all material production must move. Reality is complex. In order, therefore, to operate within it, is it still possible to approach reality from a single author's intervention? Is it still possible to put forward architectures that respond to reality from a personal angle, even when such an angle touches on the artistic and the technical? And, should the personal angle not be enough, would that mean the end of architecture as the production of an individual author?

Our conception of architecture is along the lines of a basically hierarchical activity; that is, one which depends on a series of linear decisions of cause and effect. The architect conceives his design by drawing on a certain amount of information, elaborates a project which other parties subsequently realize in the actual building. From that moment on the author's abstract scheme, his design, enters into contact with reality and acts within it.

But let us imagine, instead, another possibility. We will suppose that we can conceive or address architecture not only as that linear set of activities, extending from the design to the final utilization of the building, but as a more complex, non-linear network of people, materials, information and energy which result in the constructed building. A network that is not approachable from our usual linear view of phenomena alone, but from a more complex relationship of effects, self-organized in part, impossible to be decided consciously, which would lead to a more ample and sincere view of the present-day production of architecture.

But not only the present-day. If we stop to think about the history of architecture we have learnt, we will come up against a long list of names and works, but more problematically so with anything extending beyond that linear, hierarchical vision, and that of the individual author, which we associate with a particular architectural oeuvre. Nevertheless, we know that in many cases there are other factors which are equally as important as the author's intervention, even though it is that alone which might have endured. The rapport with the client, a fixed location, the involvement of other material agencies, etc. Although it may not seem so, the history of architecture is by no means merely the sum of authors and their works.

While the debate about ideas on the design of architecture has become ever more complex over the years, that complexity has not been adequately applied to the actual processes of production and to the relationship between the architect and reality. Reality is highly complex and it is important to elaborate increasingly complex models for translating these phenomena into given forms. Meanwhile, the architect's activity continues being an author's activity, vertical, categorical and totally hierarchical, one that tends to impose these models on reality through his designs.

Let us introduce, then, that new variable into the discussion. We will contend that the computerization of the world brings us the data necessary to make this possible.

The production of architecture is no longer a material production solely determined by the human factor, but is partly developed according to dynamics which extend beyond the absolute control of the people who conceive buildings.

The development of new models of reality and the potential capacity for calculating material procedures have introduced this new and different quality. The architect is no longer the unique author, the sole master of the form.

This does not imply, however, the absolute negation of the architect as author, but only a transformation of his status. Architecture is the material production of objects, and such production – like any other – must be considered as a complex interaction of flows of information, matter and energy, over and above the mere linear sum of the parts – human, material or categorical – which comprise up.

Endophysics, a recent branch of physics, introduces the idea that our perception of reality is a question of interfaces. The interface as a model, or as a perception, of reality. Objective reality does not exist, since our relative position within reality annuls any absolute relationship to it. Endophysics relativises our relationship to the world by considering that the external position of an observer is only possible in the shape of a model, and is never within reality itself. According to Gödel's [1] theorem of indefinition, it is only from outside a complex universe that it is possible to give a complete description of it. Applied to architecture, this endophysical idea forces us to the conclusion that our view of reality is a question of interfaces.

"The world changes in relation to our interfaces with it. The limits of the world are the limits of our interface. We do not interact with the reality of the world, we do so with its interface." Peter Weibel [2]

And so we will consider architecture as an interface, and therefore the transformation of reality as a transformation of the architectural interface. We will posit, then, an alternative view of the history of architecture as an interface with the world. We can describe many historical phenomena in a different way; in relation to information and to interaction, for example. Or architecture's transformation from classical grammar to modern abstraction, for instance.
In classical architecture the interaction of the architect was practically nil and that of the user non-existent. The architect made use of a series of aesthetic invariants which he applied by following equally invariant grammars. Let's say that the author's rare variations on that system are those which have actually subsisted until our own times as decisive moments in the history of classical architecture. That is, the architectural interface was a barely interactive and highly hierarchized method.
When the transformation of the medium takes place through abstraction, the architectural

interface gains in interactivity, both for the architect and for the user. The architect acquires a lot of autonomy in his activity — his activity is much more interactive with the medium — because form ceases to ultimately depend on a rigid formal or aesthetic syntax. And the user equally gains, too, in his capacity for interaction. Not as much as the architect, but now his perception, the perception the user has of a building, becomes an important factor of the architecture. The user interacts with modern architecture through his perception of the object, his changing vision of the object.

Relative to this vision of architecture as interface, the next step is in the increase of interaction, not on the part of the architect — who has already acquired complete autonomy within modern architecture —, but on the part of factors external to the author, like the data of reality itself or the increased interactivity of potential users. That is, *in the interface of any architecture coming after modernity the interaction of other factors external to the architect himself increases.*

Information

But in what way? How can the interaction of other factors external to the architect increase? We come back once more to the comparison between the modern and the postmodern idea. One of the basic characteristics of the change lies in the perception of speed. According to Paul Virilio, classical modern society is founded on a physically perceptible mechanical speed, such as fascinated the Futurists at the beginning of the 20th century. In architecture the entire production of architectonic objects until far into the century — even today — is still based on this perception of time and space. The object is created a priori by the architect as a message impermeable, to all intents and purposes, to the interaction of the perceiver, if this is not simply through his perception: a passive activity. Considering architecture as the former interface, the user's interaction — albeit fundamental — is practically nil.

Postmodern speed, on the other hand, is absolute. It is the speed of information, the speed of light. In what way can the perception or the interaction of the architectonic message change in an environment of instantaneous speed? Obviously this does not entail an acceleration in the perception of architecture to unimaginable speeds, but a change in the nature of the interface of the architecture. If the interactivity between architect and user was practically nil before, the tendency would now be towards an ever-growing increase in the interactivity of both. The outcome of absolute speed is simultaneous space and time. *In the simultaneity of space and time information becomes the relational medium between both parties, by means of which interactivity increases. That is, in a postmodern design process the architect and the user 'interact' through information, and this capacity for interaction is each time greater.*

"The aesthetics of interactivity are based on action much more than on visual perception." Dick Rijken [3]

This transformational and generic notion of the potential of information society and of the interactive dimension is nothing new. From the founders of cybernetics, such as Norbert Wiener [4], to the inspired thinking of Marshall McLuhan, many voices have warned of the dangers that the technological implementation and the ever-increasing, unstoppable development of global information may involve. Certain philosophical positions exist today that argue against the definitive and basic destructiveness provoked by the era of information, of the interaction or the final implanting of an absolute, and trans-ideological, reality on the world. In *The Perfect Crime*, for example, J. Baudrillard [5] makes no bones about the final conclusion of this tendency towards electronic, computer or virtual dissolution. For Baudrillard, the world has already committed the crime of exterminating illusion. Magic has disappeared, because the entire history of humanity up to now has been the history of the progressive 'unmasking', extermination and crime of the illusion through a simulation effect, which is precisely a gigantic enterprise of disillusion to the profit of an absolutely real world.

"We live in the illusion that the real is what is most lacking, when the opposite is the case: reality has reached its extreme. By dint of technical prowess, we have attained such a degree of reality and objectivity that we can even speak of an excess of reality, leaving us much more anxious and disconcerted than the lack of reality, which we were at least able to compensate for with utopia and the imaginary, while for the excess of reality there is no compensation or alternative."

"Modernity as a whole has had the advent of this real world as its goal, the freeing of men and of real energies, focused on the objective transformation of the world, and extending beyond all the illusions whose critical analysis nourished philosophy and praxis. Today the world is more real than we imagined. An inversion of real and rational data has been produced by their own fulfilment."

"with virtual reality and its consequences, we have gone over to technique as the ultimate phenomenon. Beyond this there is no reversibility, no traces, not even nostalgia for an earlier world. The hypothesis is that of irreversible disappearance, within the purest logic of the species. That of an absolutely real world in which we would have succombed to the temptation of leaving no traces."

For P. Virilio [6], in *The Information Bomb,* the danger is not in information per se, but in interactivity and its dimension as global cybernetic feedback in real, instantaneous time.

"Interactivity is to information what radioactivity is to energy: a colossal force."

"Today's politicians don't understand technique, techno-scientific potential and globalization. The real power is held by the market's feudal barons: the Gateses, Murdochs and Soroses."

The computerization of procedures and the interaction implicit in them cannot, for all that, be rejected out of hand. The computerization of the world is neither good nor bad. It simply is. Utopian messages or regressing to anachronistic positions serve for nothing in an era in which ideas are slower moving than reality itself. In his essay *Fresh Conservatism*, Roemer van Toorn [7] describes the general situation — general for a whole generation — of contemporary art and culture as it flails about between mere uncritical acceptance and the transcending of today's hyper-real, alienating state of affairs. According to Van Toorn, the danger inherent in such a tightrope situation is that its apparently uninhibited, novel and innovatory attitude towards reality only masks the destructive potential of the forces Virilio describes. Therein lies the risk. There is no earlier formula on which to base oneself. The only possible innovative action, for all that, is to accept and assimilate the situation, not reject it. *And this by rediscovering the artistic dimension — a different dimension —, the authentic dimension of postmodern architecture in the computer era, of a trans-aesthetic architecture,* of which the MVRDV scheme for VPRO is an implicit example. A dimension that can lead to curious effects, once the information on a building like the VPRO building has become diffused in the global information sphere. For example, what Van Toorn says about the building has great similarity to the plot of the first story appearing in the final part of the book.

"The insatiable communicator, like some contemporary globetrotter moving from one spectacle to another with his sensory feelers constantly alert, can find peace here."

Is Van Toorn referring in his commentary to Benito Navalón Molina, perhaps? [8]

In-form-ation

The main consequence of architecture as the interface of computerized reality is that there is a direct relationship between information and form.

In the postmodern project, or that of secondary computer abstraction, information 'takes on' a shape, and this discovery is the most fascinating achievement of the architectural scheme implemented by MVRDV.

Unlike modern abstraction, which tends to disengage the form of any concrete syntactic meaning, postmodern secondary abstraction adopts the data of reality and transforms them into buildable matter. Architecture, then, is no longer a "knowing game of pure, light-filled volumes," but an "effective recycling of real data into buildable matter." Let's consider that possibility of converting information into matter. The idea is barely thirty years old. Our current reality is still in a hybrid state — up to a point it is still more mechanical than computerized — but there's nothing to suggest that the electronic computerization of the world might not increase to the point of taking the place of the mechanization which has typified the century that's drawing to a close.

There exist an infinite number of procedures which can serve as an example of that current hybrid condition. Let's consider, for instance, one example of physical transformation that is directly dependent on information: urban mobility. An application which may make architects think of the physical application certain computerized procedures can have on reality. When an architect or town planner considers mobility, he does so by immediately thinking of some kind of physical support — a medium, in short — that renders such mobility possible. In support terms, the physical supports of a visible infrastructure would be considered along with roads, but also the invisible, and equally physical, infrastructures of the communication networks that are similarly responsible for transforming post-industrial urban mobility.

That is a fact, no doubt about it. But it is also a fact that **our contemporary hybrid situation — one that is more ecologico-informational than mechanical — introduces new variables which combine with that physical idea** — visible or invisible —, to make any investigation — and not just as physical action alone — of mobility more interesting.

Faced with the problems caused by saturation, consumerism and environmental degradation, an alternative form of property develops. With car-sharing — or multi-ownership — the energy, economic and spatial expenditure of many cars with many individual owners is converted into less cars, plus the computer-generated information necessary for having access to them at any one moment. Unlike renting, a monthly subscription allows the co-owner to have access to a car in a series of fixed city locations at any moment of the year. Each shared car thus replaces five or ten individual cars.

A mass of combustion engines is converted into less engines, and into information. As for urban mobility, massive combustion gradually gives way to less combustion, backed up by electronics. What is now happening with the actual automobile engine is also happening with mobility as a social or urban factor. **The transformation of means from the 'purely solid' to the 'computerized' is obvious, even though it's difficult at times for us to understand this.**

This transformation is important in that it enables us to entertain the possibility of understanding the design and production processes of architects as something non-linear. A few years ago Manuel de Landa [9] speculated on the possibility of using self-organizing logics for current traffic systems which wouldn't depend on vertical structures of centralized decision-making.

"The real application of artificial intelligence depends on an interaction with non-linear dynamics. This means that invisible computerization needs to be applied for the support and for the development of self-organizing networks of human production." Manuel de Landa

The authentically transformative dimension of MVRDV's 'computer' approach to the design of architecture lies there. MVRDV designs with a *logic according to which complex reality is broken down into simple, quantifiable data which can be readily re-elaborated into buildable matter.* The design process, then, isn't rooted in voluntary modern abstraction, but in a computer — 'binary' — abstraction of reality. The curious and fascinating thing about such a procedure, as Stan Allen [10] has pointed out, is that despite the apparently impersonal automation of the procedure the result is not in the least automatic. Despite having "decodified complex reality into bits of LEGO" and having recombined it anew, there is no echo in the edified building of this process. In MVRDV's own commentaries, they wisely speak of contents, phenomena, never of the technical or procedural support which makes these possible. For example, in the case of VPRO the main challenge consisted in 'reproducing' afresh, in a new floorplan design, the whole social, environmental, ideological and operational content characteristic of VPRO, without this complicating the result with architectonic 'background noise'. The infrastructural or technical support of the building is hidden as much as possible, in such a way that the built architecture provides a mainly 'transparent' setting for VPRO's implicit content. Once again, the message is the medium.

There is a growing tendency for *postmodern design procedures to become more generic and to gradually detach themselves from their respective technical*

surroundings, since the importance of the material means by which this is generated becomes ever more relative. VPRO is also an architectural hybrid, designed 'by computer', but executed according to as-yet non-computerized procedures. Nevertheless, the media of construction – of the material production of the architecture – are being progressively computerized and added to the common fund of information on which the architect increasingly bases his work.

Haacke
It all began with a cube...

Let's go back thirty-five years in time. To New York, and the summer of 1965. Hans Haacke, a former student of the Werkakademie in Kassel, has recently settled in the United States. Before that, he has spent two years in Paris. After collaborating on the Documenta in Kassel and forming part of the 'Zero' group, he has met the most outstanding representatives of abstraction in early sixties Paris. Yves Klein, among others. In Paris he has become completely convinced that the attempts of artists like Klein to renew the mystical dimension of abstract art are heroic but useless in relation to the reality in which he lives. Haacke ends up rejecting, once and for all, the production of conventional artworks, works fixed by the artist's irrefutable subjectivity and presented in a gallery for the public's delectation. He begins to conceive the idea of elaborating systems, rather than works, which are open temporal processes. Systems in which time, energy and space assume complex, self-generating forms which do not begin functioning before being shown to the public. He dubs these 'Realzeitsysteme', or 'real-time systems'.

He calls his first system 'Condensation Cube'. It is a static cube of plexiglass which he partially fills with water. With the difference of temperature between inside and outside, the walls of the transparent cube start to cover over with tiny droplets caused by the condensation of the water. "The condensation process continues," he writes, "and the cube's appearance slowly changes, without ever repeating itself. Its condition is similar to that of a living organism which reacts flexibly towards its environment. The image of the condensation cannot be predicted with any certainty; depending on statistical changes, it varies. I like that freedom." Haacke is increasingly taken with cybernetics as a model for understanding complex structures of behavior. Growing out of the military-scientific developments of the Cold War, this new science is devoted to studying information and assessing its use in artificial machines. 'Condensation Cube' is the first of Haacke's 'real time' physical systems. He will continue experimenting in this area until the end of the 70s. 'Wave' (1965), 'Blue Sail' (1965) and 'Circulation' (1969) are still physical systems of water or air. 'Ant Coop' (1969) and 'Chickens Hatching' (1969) are already animal systems. He writes about the aim of the systems:

"... to create something which gives in to the environment, which reacts, changes, is unstable...

... to create something indeterminate, which is always perceived differently, with a form that is not accurately predictable...

... to create something that cannot 'function' without the help of the environment...

... to create something that responds to light and to changes of temperature, is sensitive to air currents, with a functioning that depends on the forces of gravity...

... to create something that the 'spectator' can manipulate, can bring to life through his actions...

... to create something that evolves in time and allows the 'spectator' to experience time...

... to articulate something Natural... "

Haacke gradually supplants his laboratory-style 'real-time systems' — first physical, then natural and animal — with social and economic human systems. He first creates a series of installation-surveys called 'Polls', and in 1971 invents a 'real-time social system' called 'Shapolsky et al. Manhattan Real Estate Holdings, as of 1 May 1971'. This consists of an exhaustive study, using property registration data, of the speculative practices of a number of companies developing a Manhattan neighborhood. The situation criticized there drew attention to the fraudulent activities of the Shapolsky development group and their effects on the urban form of the Lower East Side. This exhibition was intended for the Guggenheim Museum, but was mysteriously withdrawn six weeks before its opening. [11]

Hans Haacke's 'real-time systems' are, then, a first stab at making formal use of information. Haacke helps us grasp the potential of understanding information as the possible raw material of form, but also of understanding that, *beyond its apparent transparency, the use of data throws up readings that are much more polemical than what actual artistic practice appears to show. Once again, the meanings derived from the merely apparent mechanical use of information go way beyond the activity itself, and right there is where the trans-artistic idea of Haacke's art, or the architecture of murdu, lies in wait.*

mvrdv

Twenty-six years after Haacke's 'real-time social system', Winy Maas, a member of MVRDV, measures the effects of town planning for the masses and calls these 'datascapes'. [12] This involves carefully observing the social, economic, speculative and other causes that generate specific changes in urban form.

"These phenomena occur according to apparently disorganized patterns whose almost total chaos possesses hidden logics enabling 'densities' to emerge from among the immense and indifferent mass of objects. Such densities are revealed on being sublimated in a set of given circumstances or maximized limitations assumed in advance. Densities that emerge in the form of the data landscapes below them."

MVRDV's architecture has already been analysed on a number of occasions. In their work, MVRDV openly reject artistic subjectivity and replace it with scientific analysis. Their approach — more analytic than artistic — to the designing of architecture has been considered, in all its forms, as basically an authorial option. Different and more suggestive than others, but authorial all the same. This is true in part, but it is clear that it has in turn opened a door onto a different kind of architectural method. This is not just the work of more architects, but an architecture of a different — partly different — kind to authorial architecture. And with it, a door has also opened onto the possibility of tackling the complexities of the processes of current reality in a non-linear way.

For MVRDV reality is already sufficiently complex in itself, without adding further levels of complexity to it on which to base the purposive activity of architecture. If we look at current debate, what we have before us is a vast panorama of ongoing self-justification.

The basic reasons for planning go: the more complex it is, the better. The rationale behind a work is almost as important as the work itself. In an essay on MVRDV, Stan Allen pinpointed what he considers the fundamental reasons for the creative power of their work. Its force resides precisely in the lack of force their theory has. That is, in the absence of theory. In the automatic irrefutability of their procedures. Instead of going back to the origins of the universe to explain their work — which would amount to demonstrating a classical modern ambition — it suffices for them not to have a theoretical explanation for what they do: for them reality suffices to explain it. Winy Maas is proud of this. Any of the forms 'processed' in the seemingly mechanical elaboration of real data is equal in complexity to the forms created personally by any of the architects who make up the current 'star system'. Despite there being an evident ambition behind this, such an ambition is transformed. The architecture of the information era is based on the dissolution of the architectural message in the actual medium.

There is no established aesthetic, or ordained typological process, or a priori determining factor. The only determining factors arise from the specific data of reality. Data such as the physical limitations of the building regulations, the particular characteristics of the future users — many of which can be quantatively analysed —, energy or lighting factors, etc. The design proceeds 'from below', starting with the expedient of reality, instead of proceeding 'from above'; that is, from the author's interpretive subjectivity.

One of the basic decisions of 'real-time systems' lies in establishing the boundary of the system, to what point within this it is permissible to intervene. As important as the system per se is the physical boundary within which this system is capable of functioning.

Haacke's transparent cube defines the terms of the system in the same way that mvrdv's boundaries of maximum occupation define the terms for the development of their 'real-time' design for the new VPRO headquarters in Hilversum.

Interaction
The medium and the message

One of the ideas worth re-examining is the objectual conception of architecture. The most obvious and unquestioned idea behind architecture is the fact that the act of architecting is directed towards creating built objects, buildings. Even this book, which sets out to partly question that idea, focuses on a building in order to do this. As mentioned earlier, we understand architecture in terms of objects and thus also in terms of the individuals who created those objects. Despite the fact that such an evaluation or historical vision hardly corresponds to reality, the negating of that idea can still provoke discussions of the most violent kind.

First let us establish a parallel notion, one which may shed light on this somewhat paradoxical affirmation: the notion of the medium and the message. This idea was intuited by Marshall McLuhan [13], who was led to affirm that "the medium is the message", a sublime paradox which, although restricted to communication, is useful for defining any productive act in our own information era. Through it, generically, McLuhan definitively weakened the distinction between the main focus of attention — the figure, let's say — and the seemingly irrelevant setting — the background — in which a given action unfolds. Message and

medium, figure and ground: the one is the other. Translated to architecture, the message —
the object, the figure, the building in short — is no longer understood as an object in itself,
but rather the medium in which this is generated; that is, reality. One of the characteristics,
then, of postmodern architecture is **the progressive dissolution of the architectonic
message — the design — in the medium — namely, reality.** The VPRO building
may be considered as a form which is not defined by formal invariables, but by real
variables. At least such a dimension is what makes it extraordinary, beyond the normal run
of things. At least in part, this turns it into something non-artistic, something not
submitted to the subjectivity of the artist-architect. And this is true in part.
Within the limitations imposed on it by its time, the building for VPRO is not exactly a
building. Ideally, we might consider it the transformation, in built matter, of the medium
formed by VPRO. That is to say, it wouldn't be a built object in the usual sense, but a
process open to the non-linearity of synergies which may arise, over and above the
decisions of its authors. In subjecting part of the form of the design to statistical
development, the 'message' of the building is much closer to the VPRO 'medium' that
has generated it.

WAS HET
GEBOUW

"If you really feel curious about the future, study the present."
Marshall McLuhan [14]

VPRO is a non-profitmaking organization broadcasting on a national scale. It is part of the seven major networks that make up the current broadcasting system of The Netherlands. Although it produces 66 hours of radio and 15 of television weekly, VPRO is mainly a producer of programs. This means it is neither a radio or a television station in the strict sense of the word, but that it produces programs which, instead of depending exclusively on a given medium, can be subsequently disseminated in various formats. For that reason, VPRO also produces editorial products. The most important is the information guide which is sent regularly to its subscribers. But it also produces books, and has a special department devoted to developing digital products. A staff of 350 people is structured into teams called 'program producers', which possess enormous creative and journalistic autonomy. In VPRO, instead of having studios, cameras and vast technical teams, there are only, in practical terms, people and computers. All that was said above about architecture and its transformation as a material medium also partly applies to the broadcasting media. As a medium television is also undergoing a profound physical change, a consequence of the move from analogical technology to the definitive implantation of digital media. With the new digital support the relationship between procedures within the one broadcasting station is more fluid, because there exists an abstract medium — a background — of information common to all these. VPRO Digital has long been conscious of the need to exchange the broadcasting station's current classification, based on its respective infrastructures (TV, radio and subscribers' guide), for an organizational classification based on categories of content (art/culture, people/society, science/technology, etc), as it now has its own web page (www.vpro.nl). [15] The new center takes the place of the broadcasting station's former facilities: a series of classical villas located in the middle of the town. From the very beginning this particular location has marked the identity of the station, which cannot be understood without first understanding the way in which that mixed and heterogeneous combination of both unity and independence has gradually been consolidated over the years.

VPRO is openly independent, lacking in dogmatism. Its ambition is to look at reality in as open a way as possible, by trying to adopt the maximum impartiality, even if this happens to be prejudicial to established interests and ideologies. Since its founding in 1926 this attitude has guaranteed VPRO an extremely loyal following, and also the strongest of criticism. In recent years some of its productions have caused great upsets in the public life of the Low Countries, shocks which have unleashed fierce criticism and even official sanctions, but at the same time they have also permitted the creation of levels of debate that have been highly beneficial to the public opinion of the country.

Reality always implies its particular interpretation, however objective this may claim to be. And the way of looking at reality is directly related to the cultural climate at any one moment. VPRO's main interest lies in the human factor: the fascinating nature of the individual, and his or her own possibilities and the limitations of the reality in which he or she develops. For VPRO the question of communication is basically a qualitative and not a quantitative issue. The quality of the message is more important than the quantity of the audience. A brave message indeed for those people who still seem to think that the goal of the public broadcasting media is the complete bastardisation of certain ideological and cultural issues for the masses, or to understand television or radio or any other medium as a mere instrument of power over public opinion.

A strong Dutch cultural background defined by the interaction of liberal Christianity and humanism identifies VPRO with predominant attention to the individual and to innovatory expression of all kinds.

The importance of the human factor

The emphasis on people as emancipated individuals implies that no one opinion is judged to be fixed in advance. It is necessary to know how to relativise the personal criteria of a particular opinion about things at all times. This means avoiding a simplification of approach, tackling issues with sufficient clarity and breadth, not considering more generally accepted opinions as valid because of the mere fact of their being so, but that these be analysed and evaluated in a critical spirit.

Tolerance towards those who act or speak in a different way, and concern for those who take it on themselves to adopt different kinds of behavior, has always been fundamental to a really liberal radio station. In that respect VPRO's programs attempt to encourage the direct participation of viewers and listeners, offering these the chance to draw their own conclusions and to express their own points of view. Belief in the potential of the emancipated individual brings with it a special concern for those situations in which this emancipation or freedom of action is, given a certain set of possibilities, reduced or limited. This makes VPRO feel especially implicated, and in solidarity, with those individuals or groups who are structurally or circumstantially disadvantaged, as in situations involving the unequal sharing of power or its abuse, cultural or ethical discrimination, economic oppression, etc, both locally and globally.

The new is good (until the contrary can be demonstrated)

Given its radically humanist character, its confidence in the potential of the human being, VPRO pays particular attention to all that is, or may turn out to be, innovatory. It is where there is movement that new possibilities may arise for society. If innovatory phenomena possess permanent, or only circumstantial, value is something that depends solely on practical matters. In any event, they will always be an object of special concern for the broadcasting station. This makes VPRO a pioneering, forward-looking station, be it in the social, political, ideological or religious field. The communications media, and all the more so if they originate in ethical or religious belief, tend to strengthen established thinking rather than explore what has yet to make itself known.

VPRO gives special attention to creative people and groups, to changing forms, to breaking taboos and established norms, to alternative social and cultural forms, to new ways of thinking and living. Among other things, this means granting autonomy in the overall management of the network as well as in the making of individual programs. It also experiments with new techniques and strategies of design and form, preferably in rapport with avant-garde movements in art and culture.

Despite the fact that these identifying traits do not always bear a relation to each other, the need, on the one hand, for a more relativising approach and, on the other, for a more social vision to coexist is a basic aspiration for VPRO. The tension generated between both is essential for the network. Furthermore, it isn't necessary for them to always be in contradiction with each other. To relativise doesn't mean to compromise. *Adopting a certain position doesn't mean granting an absolute value to this.*

Earlier on we were considering the system of production of architecture as an interface in which the information and the interaction of the members involved — the architect, the future user, etc — is becoming ever greater. The broadcasting media are following a similar logic, and VPRO is a clear example of the tendency towards an understanding of the media as a mixture of hierarchical decision-making and non-linear, self-functioning networks. VPRO has grown considerably over the years. *The broadcasting system in The Netherlands is based on a program quota directly linked to an audience quota, which involves considering the spectators as direct associates of the different broadcasting stations.* That is, a station will have a certain transmission time in relation to the number of spectators following and supporting it. This basically functions, then, as a democratic device: the receiving public can 'interact' with the system, depending, of course, on the degree of involvement the former wishes to have with it. VPRO even has regional meeting and advice councils for its associates, who naturally don't have the real involvement they possess in theory, mainly due to the fact that the degree of enthusiasm and sympathy for a given network does not necessarily coincide with the spectator's desire to actually involve him or herself with it. The transmission time of each network thus depends directly on the degree of acceptance the network has, based on the number of associates. It is not that each of the larger networks has its own channel, but rather that three public channels exist, for which transmission times are allotted to the different companies, seven in all. VPRO, then, has gradually gained associates, particularly from the 80s onwards. Following their first campaign for attracting these, VPRO became, with a total of 330,000 associates, a Class B broadcasting station in 1984. Seven years later, in 1991, a general media debate began on the need for a future common policy among the more like-minded stations to compete against the new, more commercial networks. VPRO feared that as a result of this competition stations would opt for greater superficiality and commercialisation in their programs, in order to push up the audience ratings and safeguard advertising contracts. Even then, VPRO didn't have sufficient clout as a category B station alongside the six other big names. In September 1991 VPRO undertook a second campaign for attracting associates, managing to almost double its quota — with some 600,000 associates — within a few weeks. Since 1992 VPRO is officially the seventh station in category A. The next step has been the creation of a major joint channel, the third public channel, formed by VPRO and the combined VARA, NPS and RVU stations. This channel is called NET 3, and will have its own campus within the Mediapark in future. [16]

This, very briefly, is the story of the vpro medium.
We offer you, below, the story of a building.
An environment that you, by putting together your own 'information'
about the subject, will go on transforming, continually, in real time.

1. Douglas R. Hofstadter, *Gödel, Escher, Bach: An eternal golden braid*. New York: Basic Books, 1979

2. Peter Weibel, "Over and Beyond the Limits of Reality". Lecture held at the Ars electronica 92 Symposium:

3. Dick Rijken, in conversation with Bart Lootsma. *Media and Architecture*. Amsterdam: VPRO and Berlage Institute, 1998

4. Norbert Wiener (1894-1964), one of the founders of cybernetics or the "science of control and communication in the animal and the machine", a science based on information theory and feedback, and how animals and machines manage to "do" things.

5. Jean Baudrillard, *Le crime parfait*. Paris: Galilee, 1995

6. Paul Virilio, *La bomba informática*

7. Roemer van Toorn, "Fresh Conservatism". Essay based on two conferences -at the Berlage Institute and the seminar *Poldergeist* of the Cooper Union- published in *Quaderns* 219 "(Re)activa"

8. Compare with the story by Rafael Reig, p. 282

9. Manuel de Landa, "Homes: meshwork or hierarchy". Essay presented during the second edition of the symposium *Doors of perception*

10. Stan Allen, "Artificial ecologies". Article on the work of MVRDV published in *El Croquis* 86

11. This installation was finally presented in the group exhibition *Art without Limit*, Memorial Art Gallery (University of Rochester, NY) in May 1972

12. Winy Maas, "Datascape". Text published in *FARMAX*. Rotterdam: 010, 1998

13. The original paradox is by Marshall McLuhan (published in Marshall & Eric McLuhan, *Laws of Media*, 1988), but its translation into parameters related to a specific contemporary architectural sensitivity is by Manuel Gausa. The paradoxes mentioned along the process of the elaboration of the VPRO project are based, above all, in his lucid reflections.

14. Marshall McLuhan, "The Best of Ideas". CBC Radio, 1967

15. www.vpro.nl

16. Information extracted from a brochure on the recent history of the broadcasting company.

INDEX

BUILDING *interface*

FICTION *interface*

'Office work' has become an umbrella term for a great variety of activities. Some of these are specific, others very much related to everyday acts such as reading, discussing, talking and so on.

Increasing numbers of people are working at home for part of the time. This means that more spaces might have a double or even triple function, since they could be used by more part-time workers. Smaller office buildings are becoming a viable prospect.

The use of computers and the increased importance of communication with its demand for teamwork offices and meeting rooms, is leading to broader buildings with more extended open plans.

Office buildings can therefore become more compact, creating space that can be used for communication or leisure purposes, which could once again encourage use of the office. These processes have been examined in the VPRO headquarters building.

For the VPRO, the Dutch 'artistic' broadcasting company, a new building means leaving the present accommodation of some eleven separate villas. Villas, which throughout the years have played a vital role in the identity of the VPRO. People who used to work in suites of rooms, attics, conservatories and bel-étages will have to find their niche in a new and truly office-like environment.

Can the present situation with its improvised use of space, which often has had an influence on the programmes that were produced there, be combined with the required 'efficiency' of a modern organization?

And can this relaxed character be reinstated even under the circumstances of enlargement? Can the metaphor of the villa still exist in our epoch?

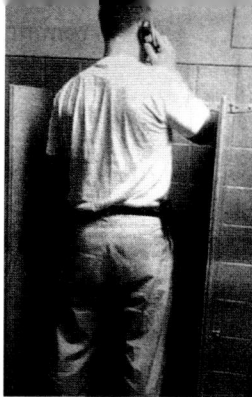

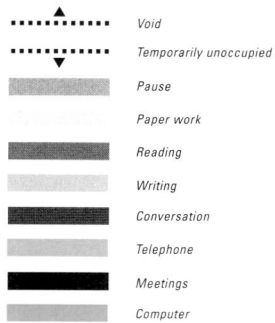

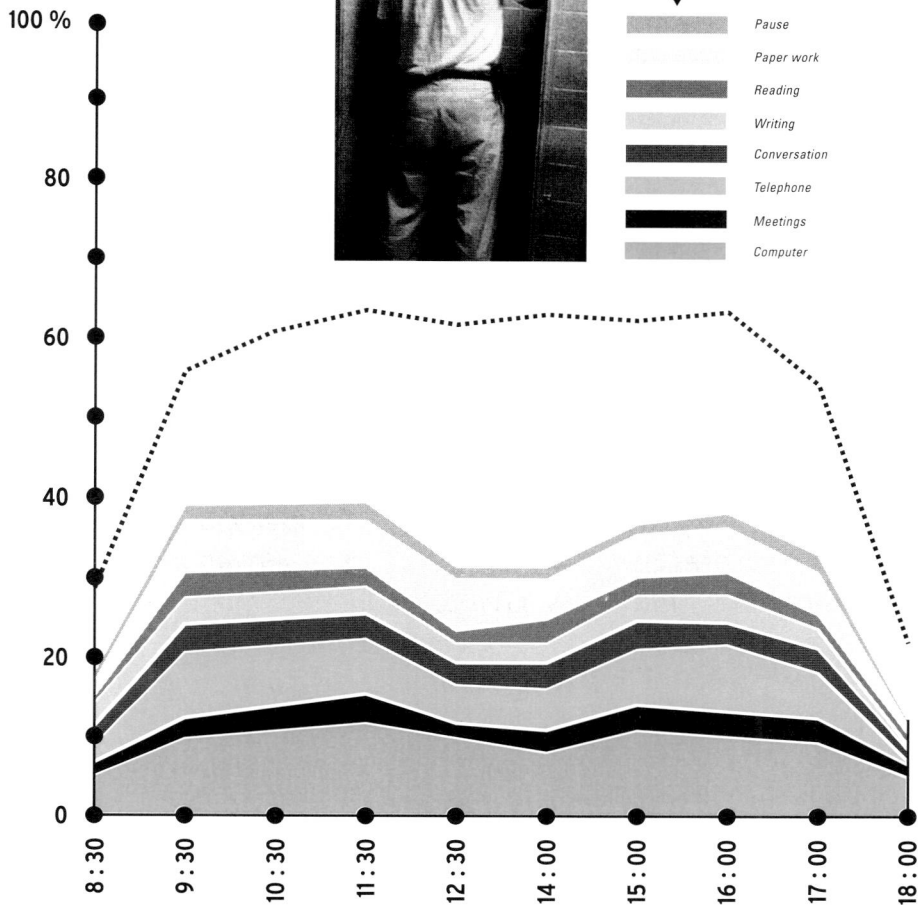

▲ .... Void

▼ .... Temporarily unoccupied

Pause

Paper work

Reading

Writing

Conversation

Telephone

Meetings

Computer

Normal ocupation of a work position

the limits
starting

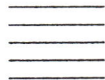

12,6 x 142,8   14,4 x 125   16,2 x 111   18 x 100

are the point

The villa can be characterized by compactness (the absence of long corridors), by stacking different types of spaces and by its relation with the surrounding landscape.

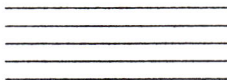

21,6 x 83,3

25 x 72

42,4 x 42,4

Possible volumes with a floor area of 9,000 m²

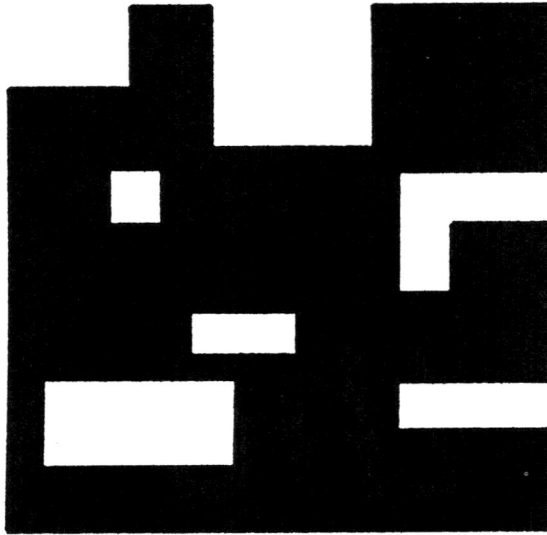

The town-planning restrictions on the site such as zoning plan boundaries and maximum building heights combined with the wish to make the smallest possible intrusion in the park resulted in possibly the deepest office building in the Netherlands.

Final volumetry. 53.7 x 53.7

A 'precision bombardment' of snake-like holes makes it possible to combine light and air with views of the surrounding.

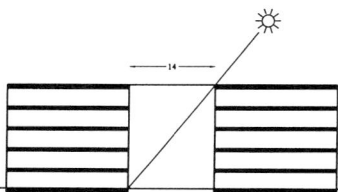

Conventional court

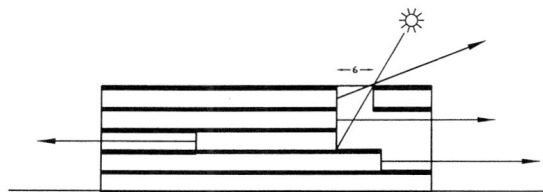

Views with terraces

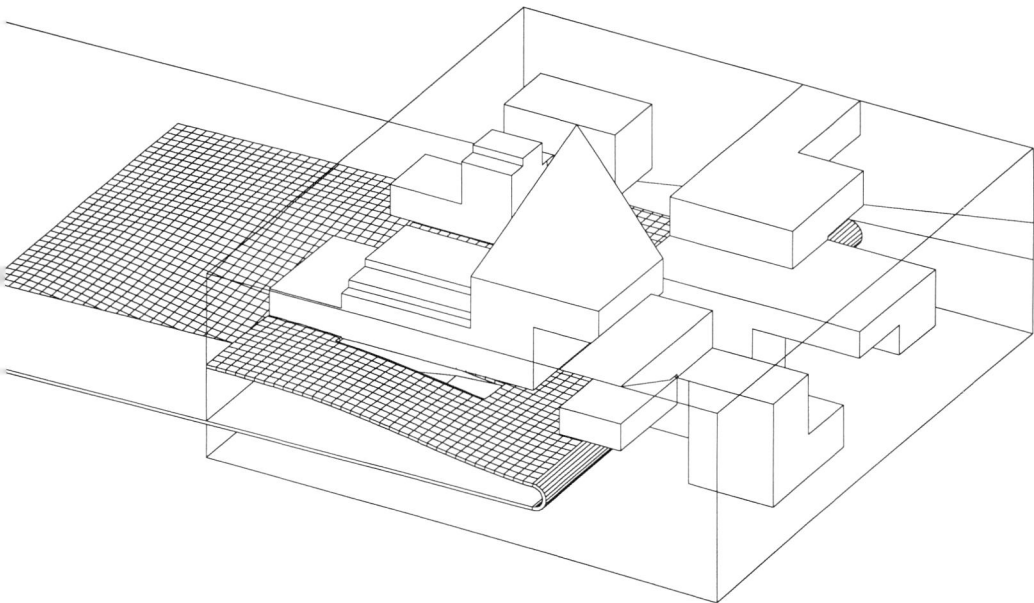

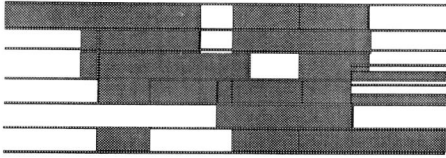

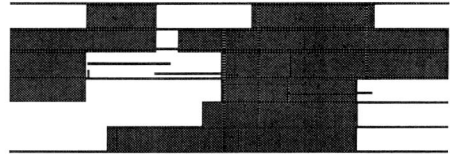

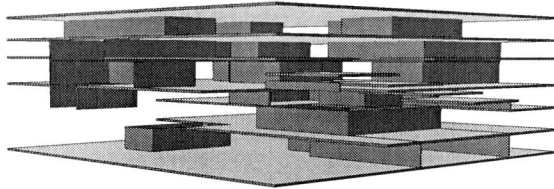

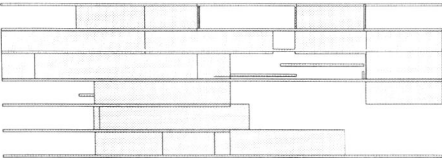

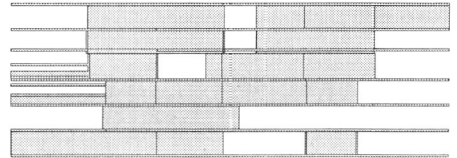

Semi-basement   Shared levels

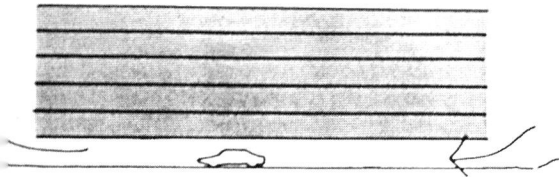

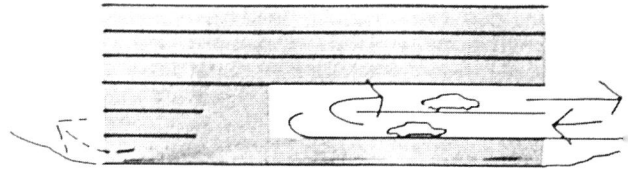

density is

The result is a literal Bürolandschaft[1] where the difference between outside and inside blurs.

1 *Office landscape*

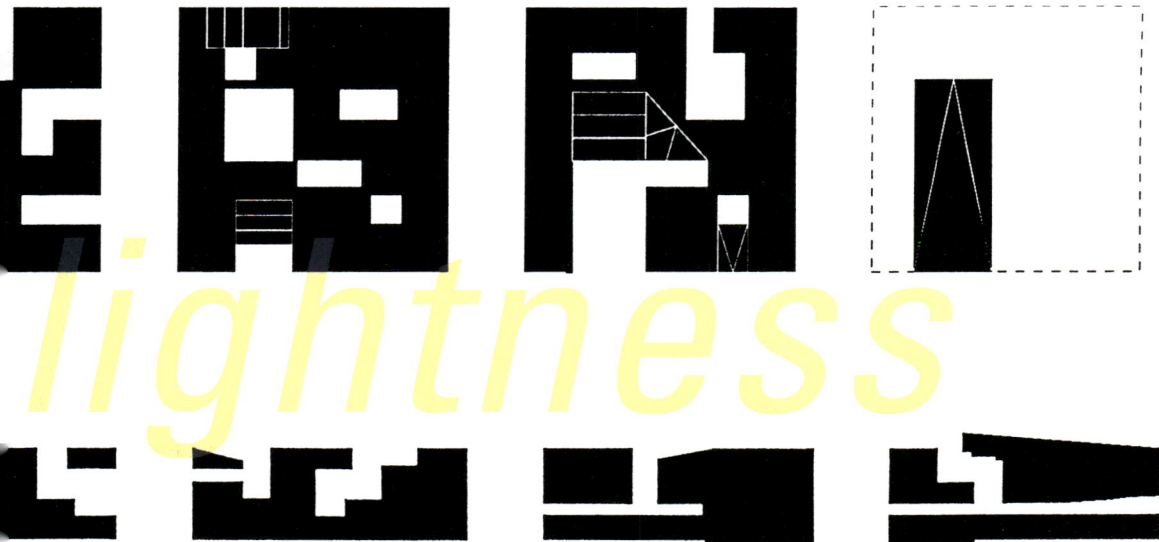

lightness

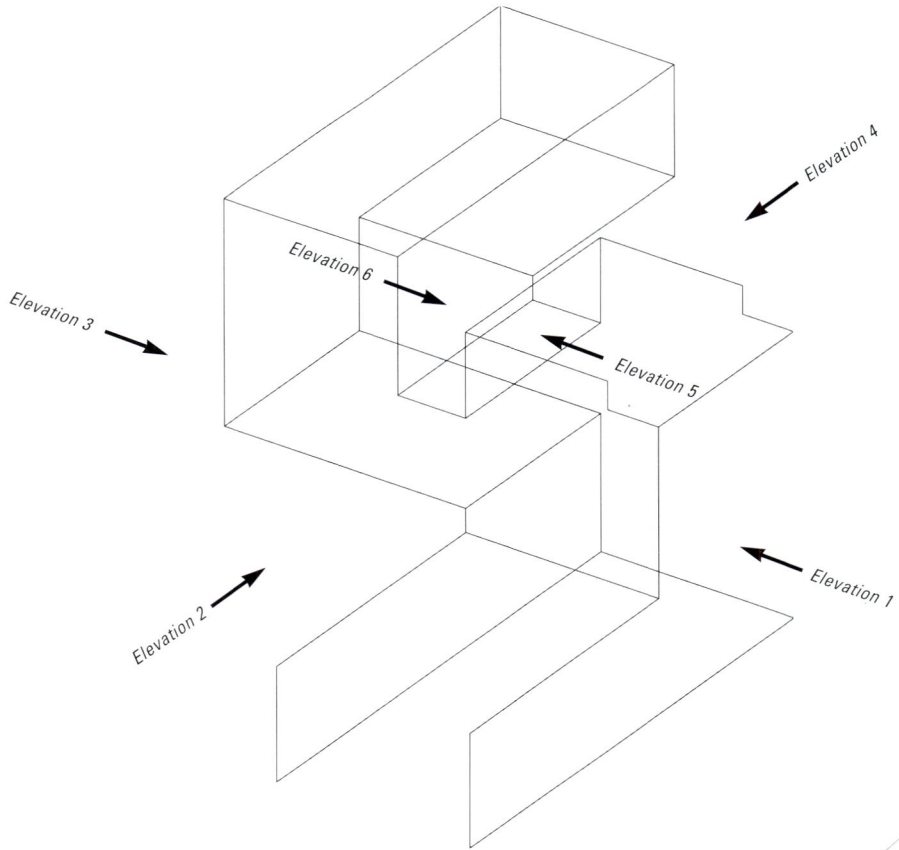

Elevation 4

Elevation 6

Elevation 3

Elevation 5

Elevation 2

Elevation 1

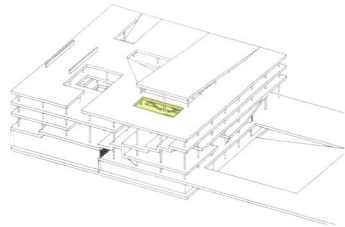

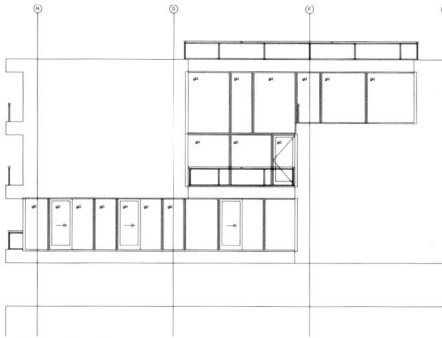

Elevation 1

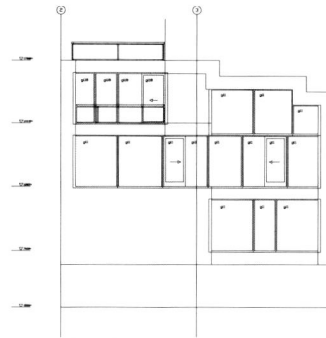

Elevation 2

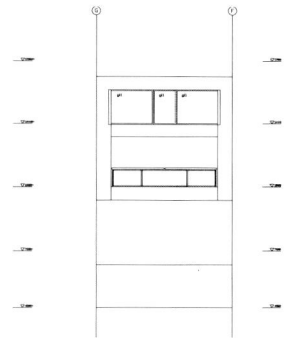

Elevation 5

Elevation 3

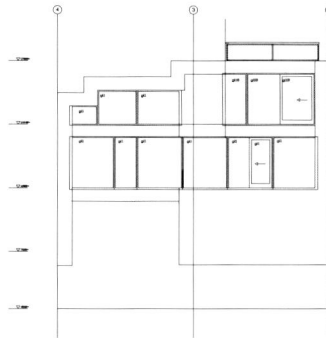

Elevation 4

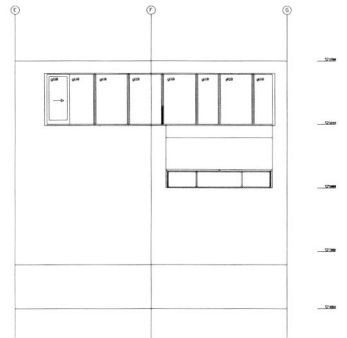

Elevation 6

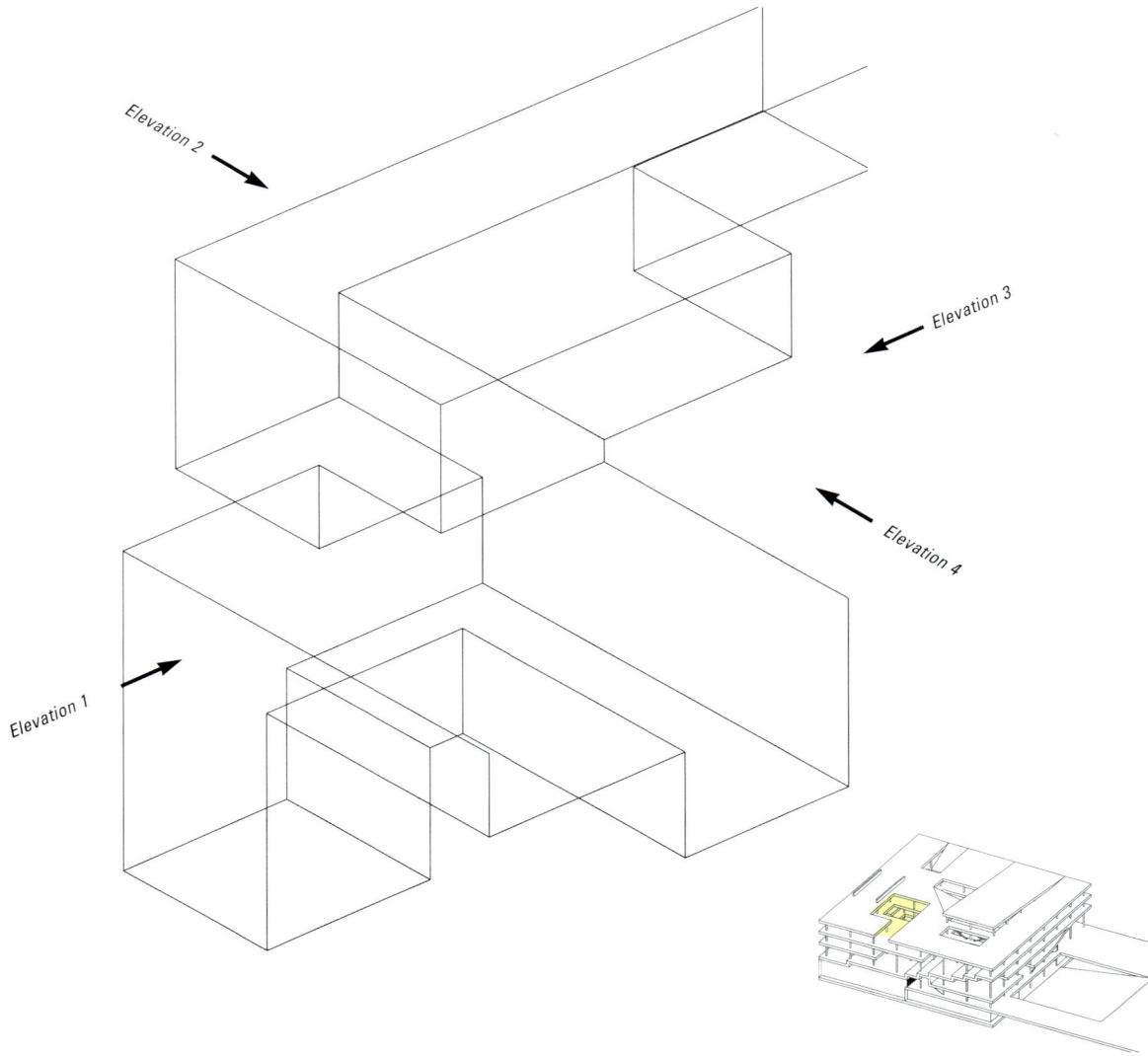

Elevation 2

Elevation 3

Elevation 4

Elevation 1

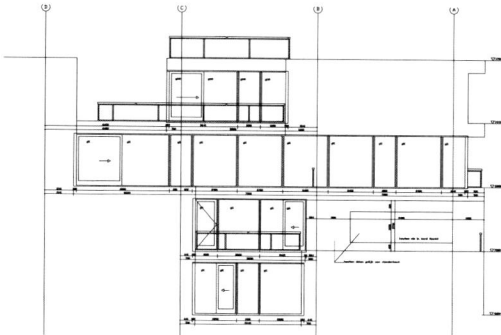

Elevation 1

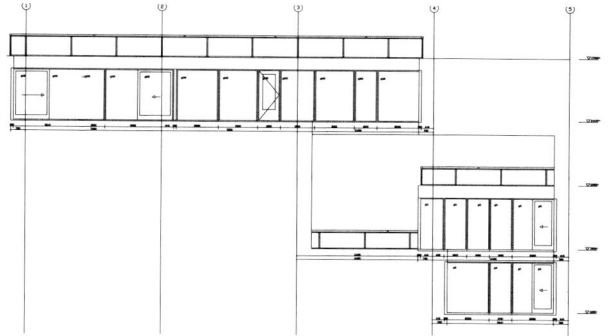

Elevation 2

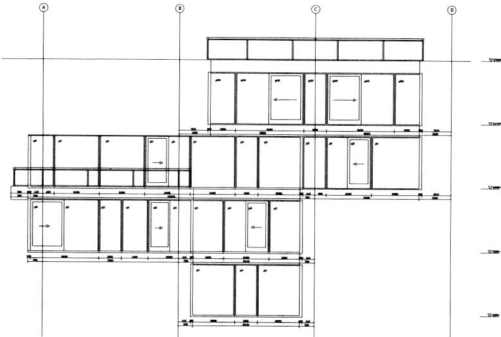

Elevation 3

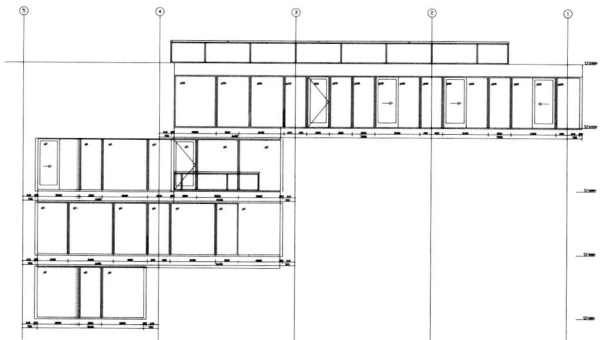

Elevation 4

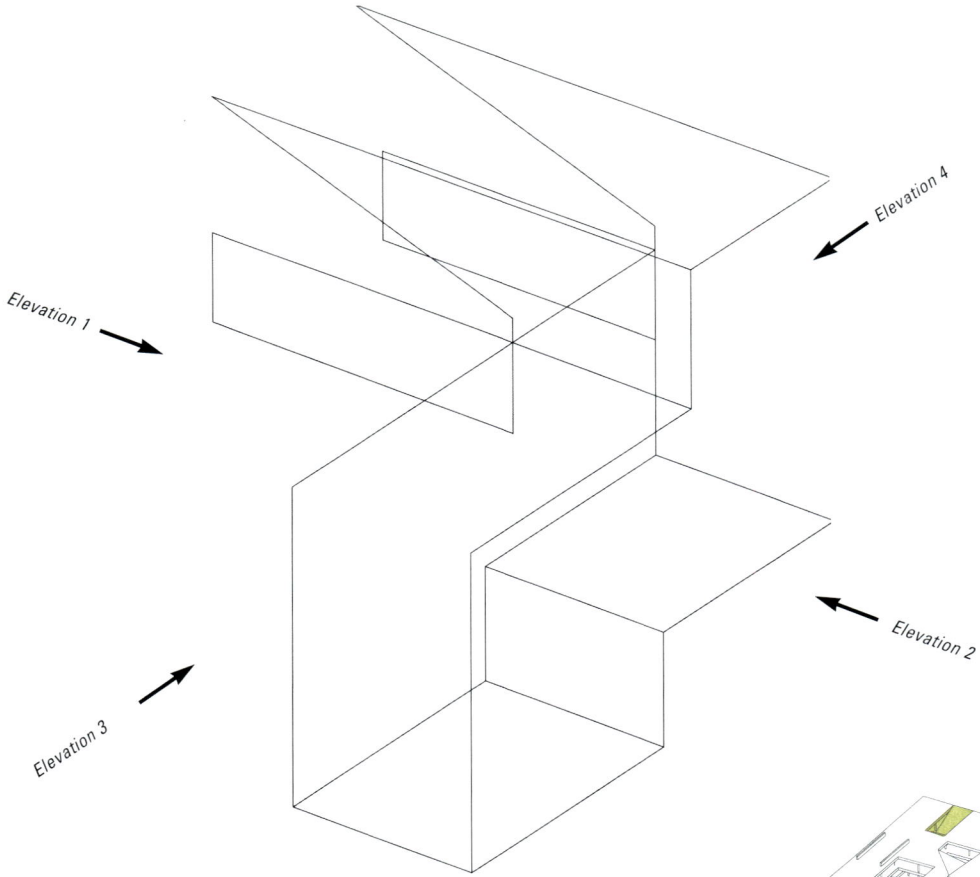

Elevation 4

Elevation 1

Elevation 2

Elevation 3

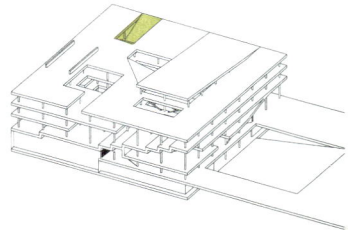

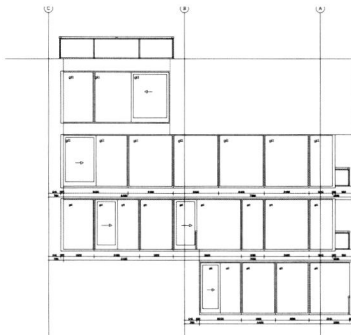

Elevation 1

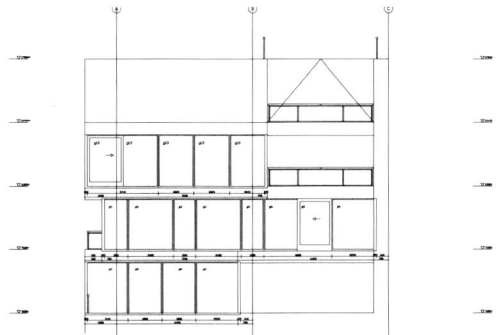

Elevation 2

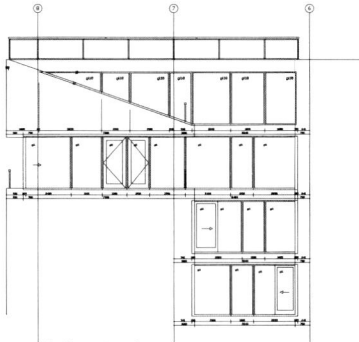

Elevation 3

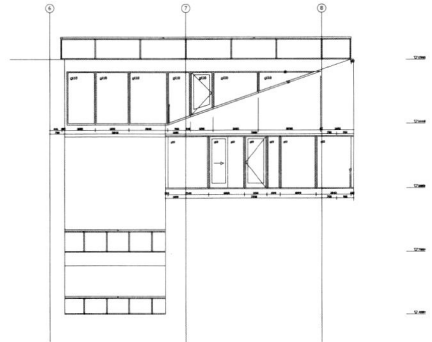

Elevation 4

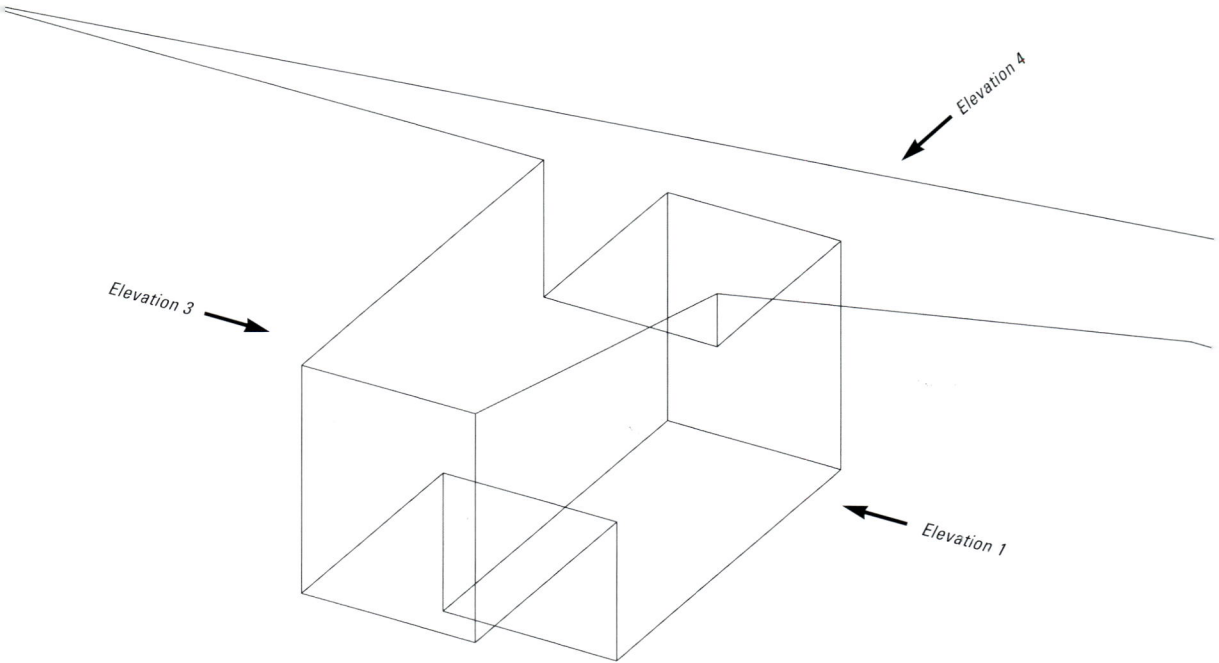

Elevation 4

Elevation 3

Elevation 1

Elevation 2

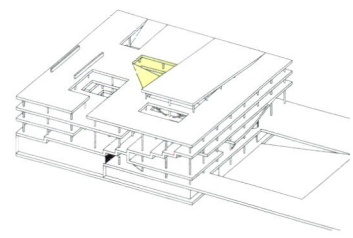

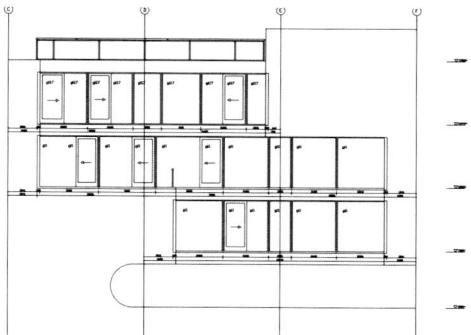

Elevation 1

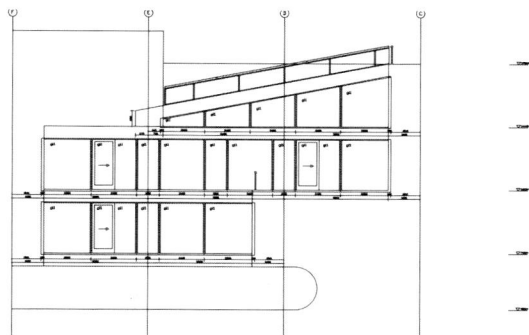

Elevation 2

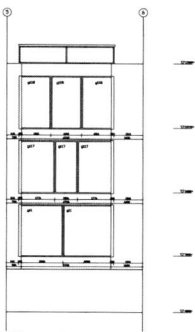

Elevation 3

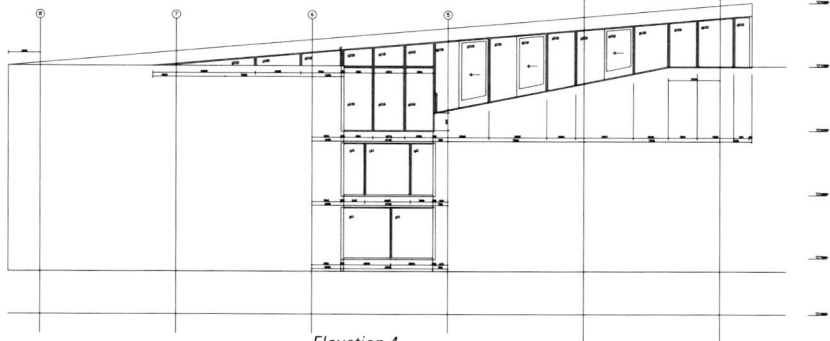

Elevation 4

the landsca
is

The existing nature of the given site is to be replaced by an elevated heather-covered roof, under which are laid out a series of 'floors' much like a geological formation.

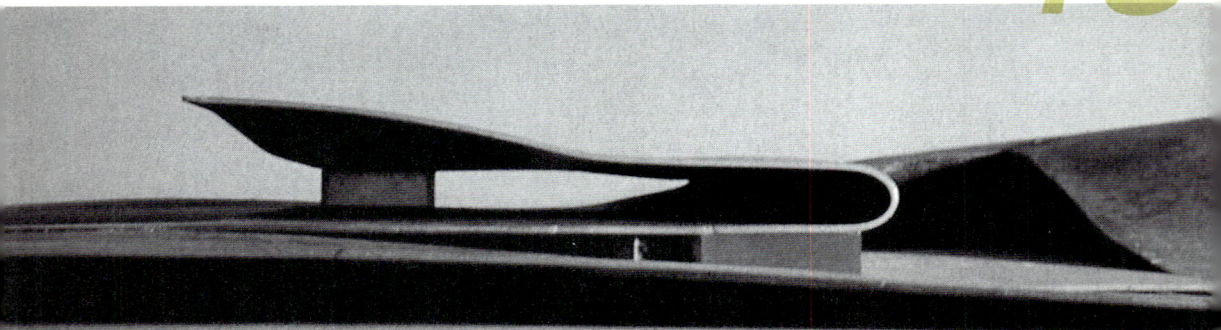

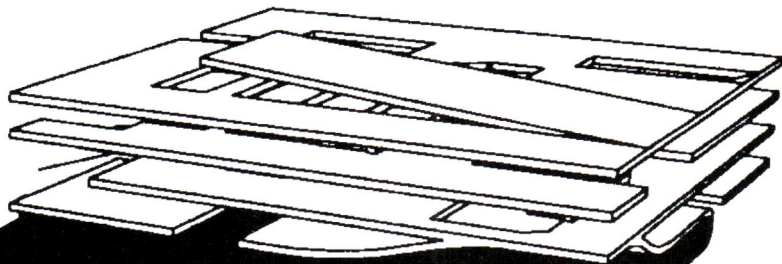

pe
the building

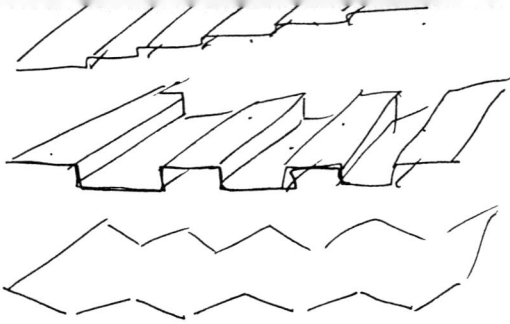

These floors are interconnected by various spatial means: ramps, monumental stairs, mini-hills, grand stairs, slopes, so forming a route leading from the surroundings up to the roof, one that aims to stimulate communication patterns within the building.

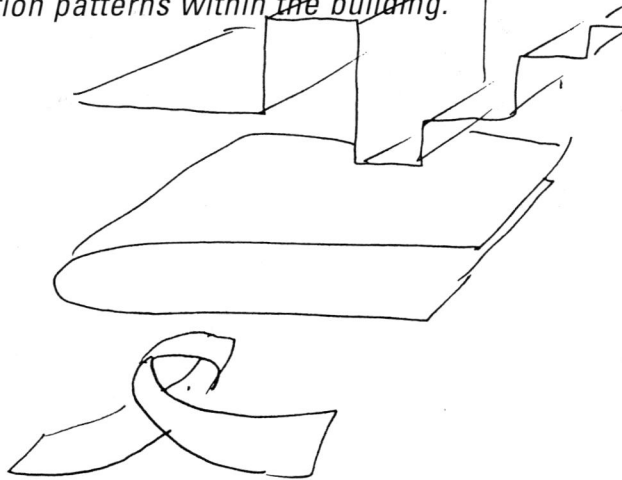

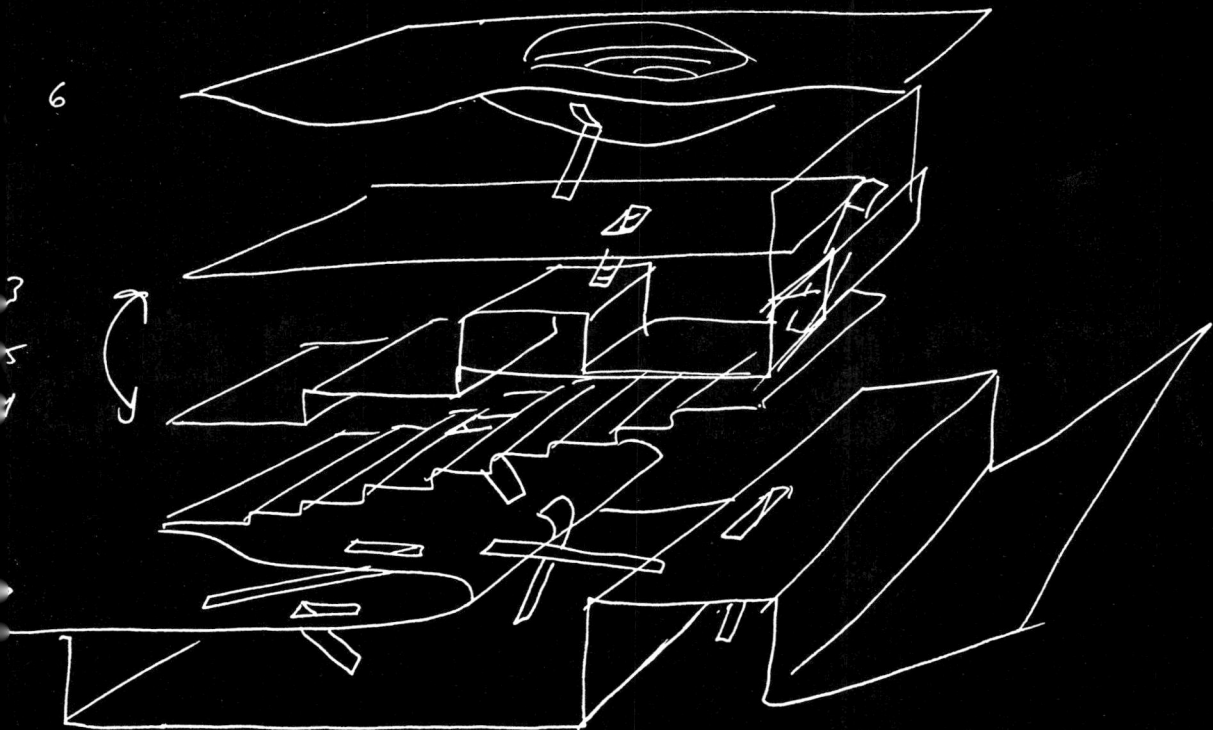

6

67

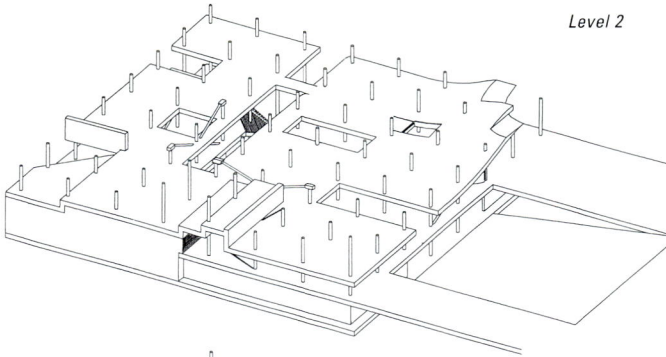

Level 2

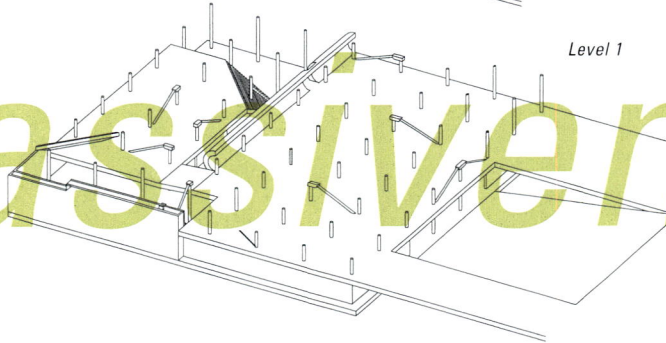

Level 1

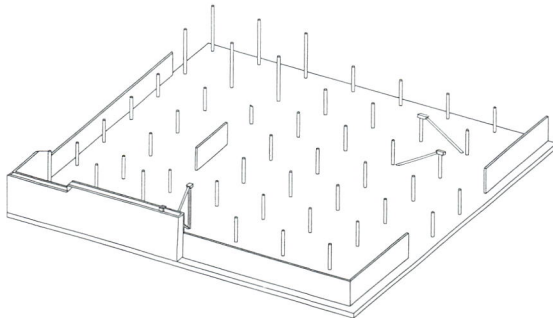

Level 0

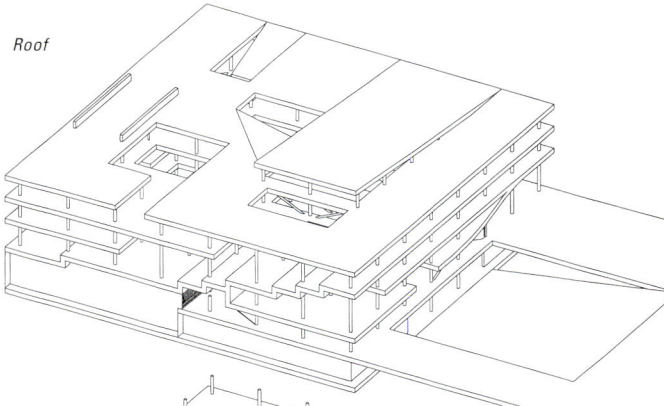

Roof

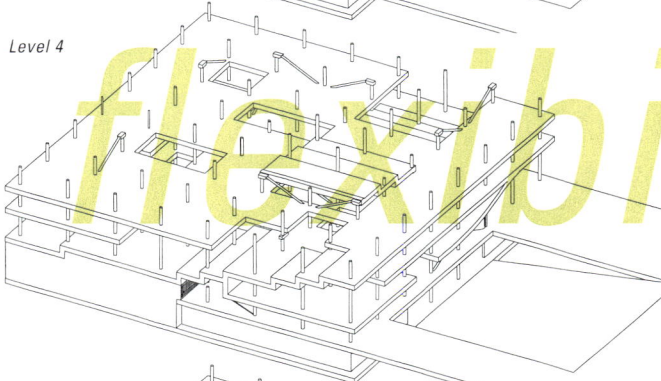

Level 4

is flexibility

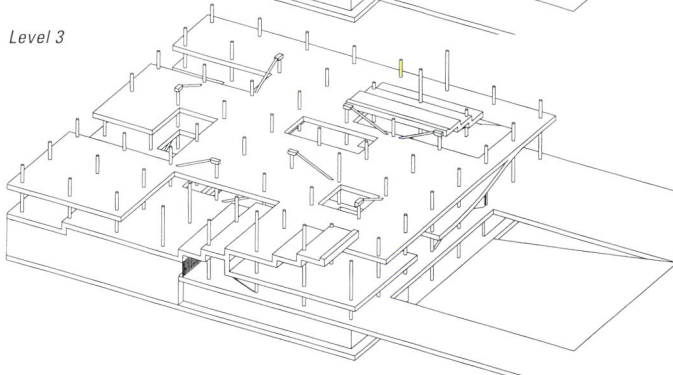

Level 3

The floors are supported by a grid of columns and stabilising props which together with the completely open elevation provide the building with the greatest possible transparency.

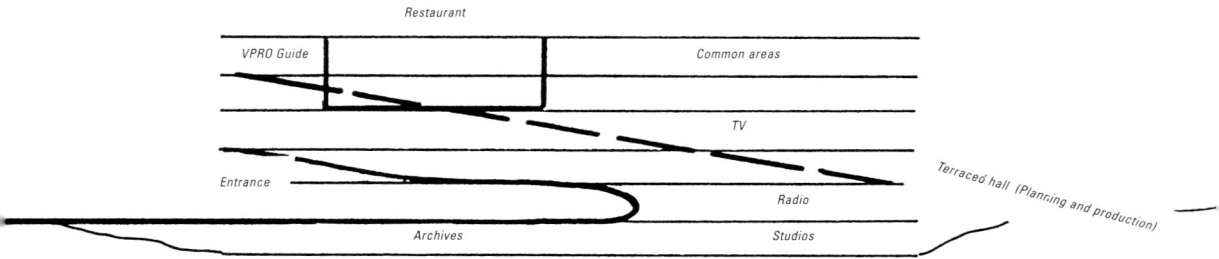

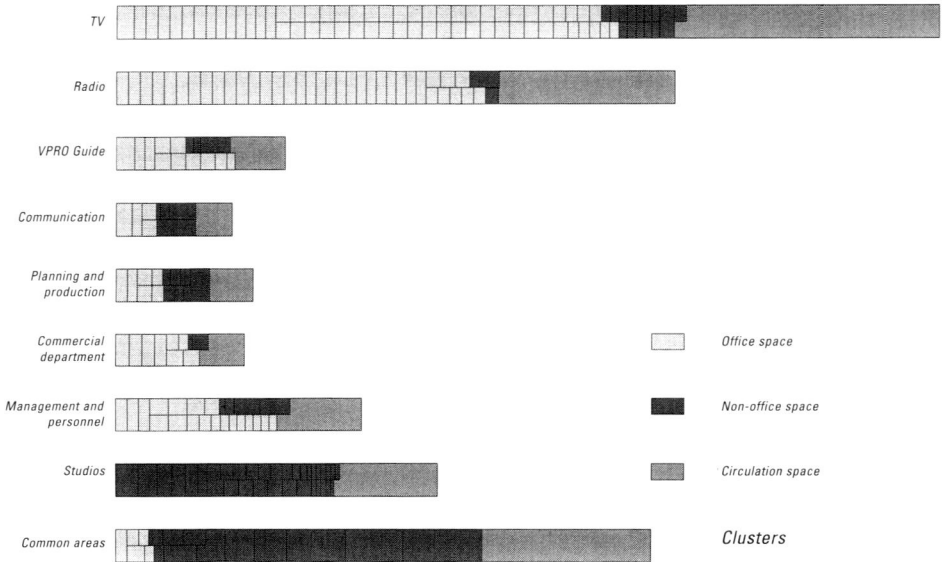

Restaurant

VPRO Guide

Common areas

TV

Entrance

Radio

Archives

Studios

Terraced hall (Planning and production)

TV

Radio

VPRO Guide

Communication

Planning and
production

Commercial
department

Management and
personnel

Studios

Common areas

Office space

Non-office space

Circulation space

Clusters

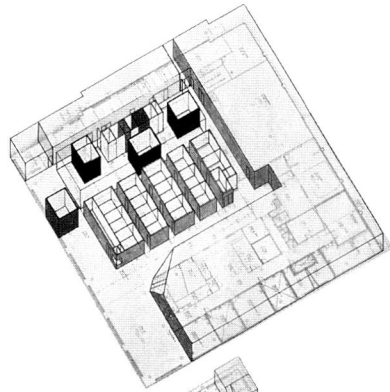

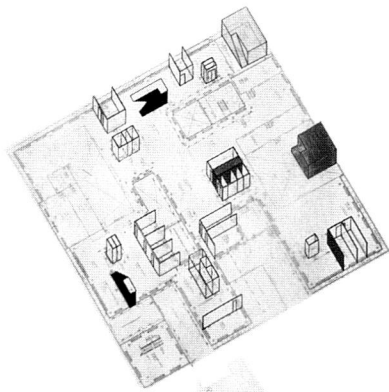

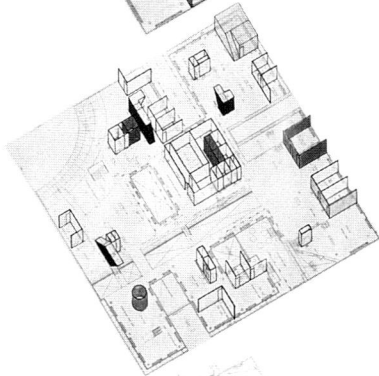

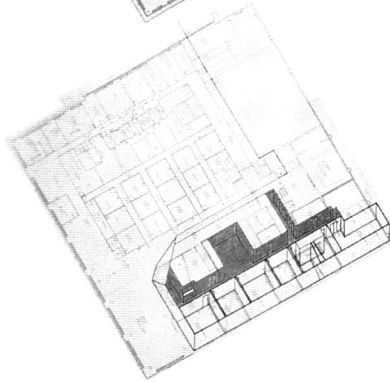

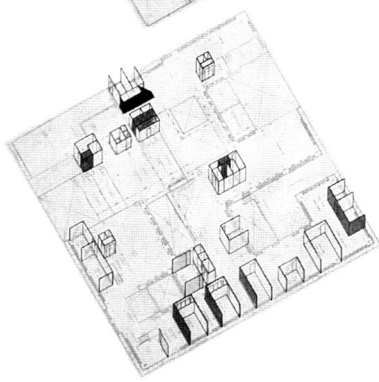

These floors can be 'urbanized' by the changing demands of the company: a range of office typologies such as the salon, attic, corridor, patio and terrace offices presents a retrospective revue of the existing villas.

71

Gross floor areas of clusters (net areas x 1.46)

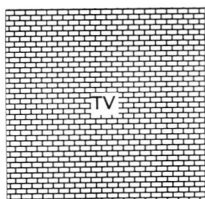

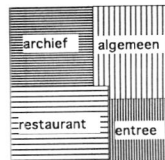

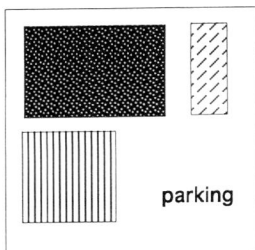

6.80

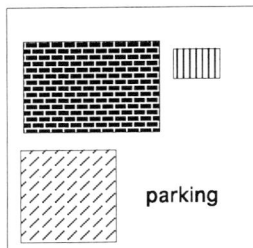

10.00

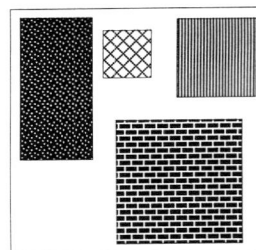

13.20

16.40

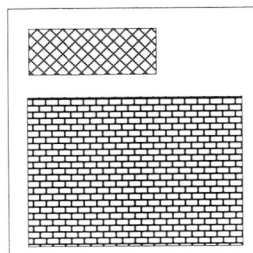

19.60

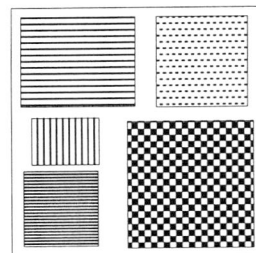

22.80

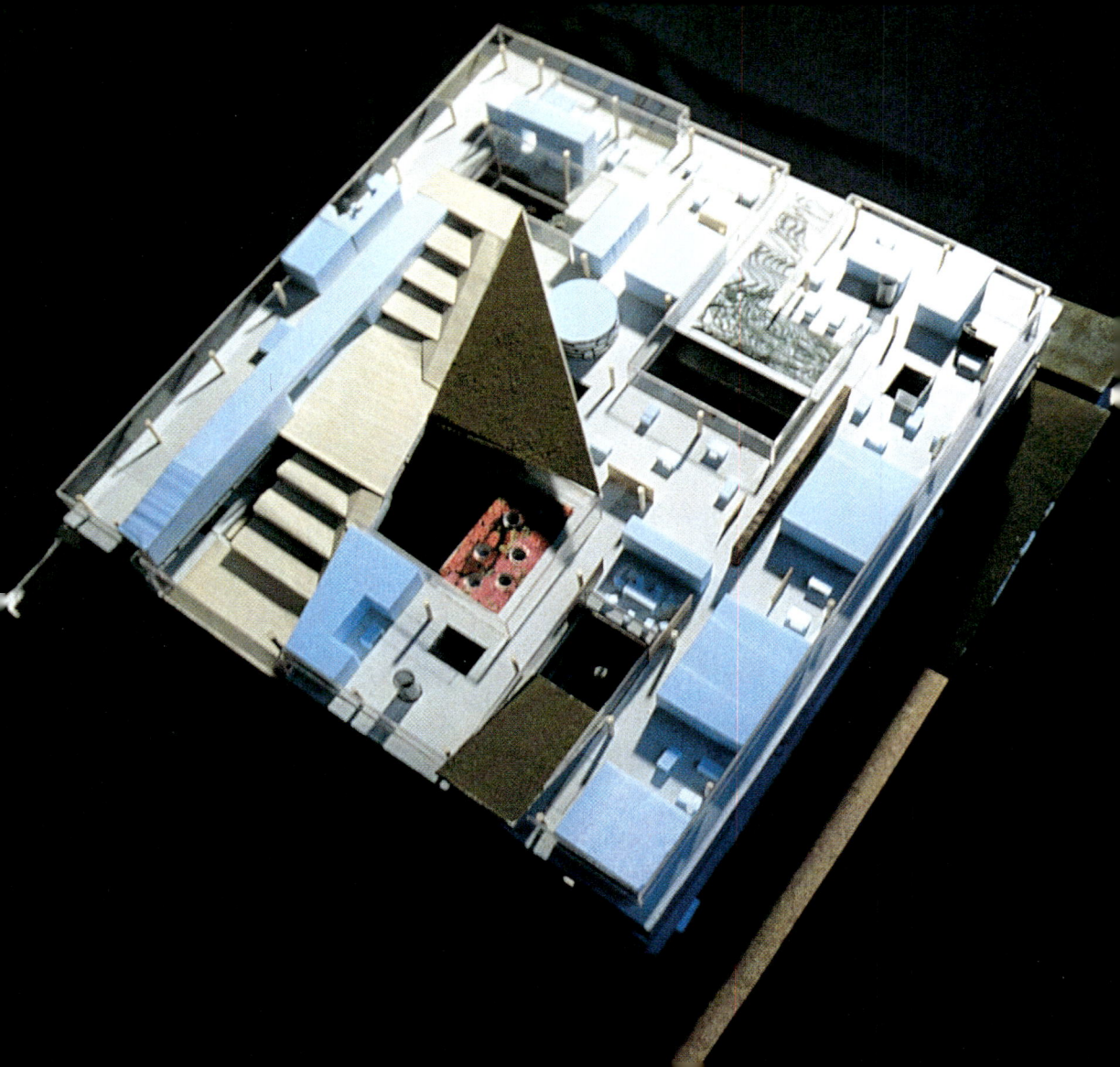

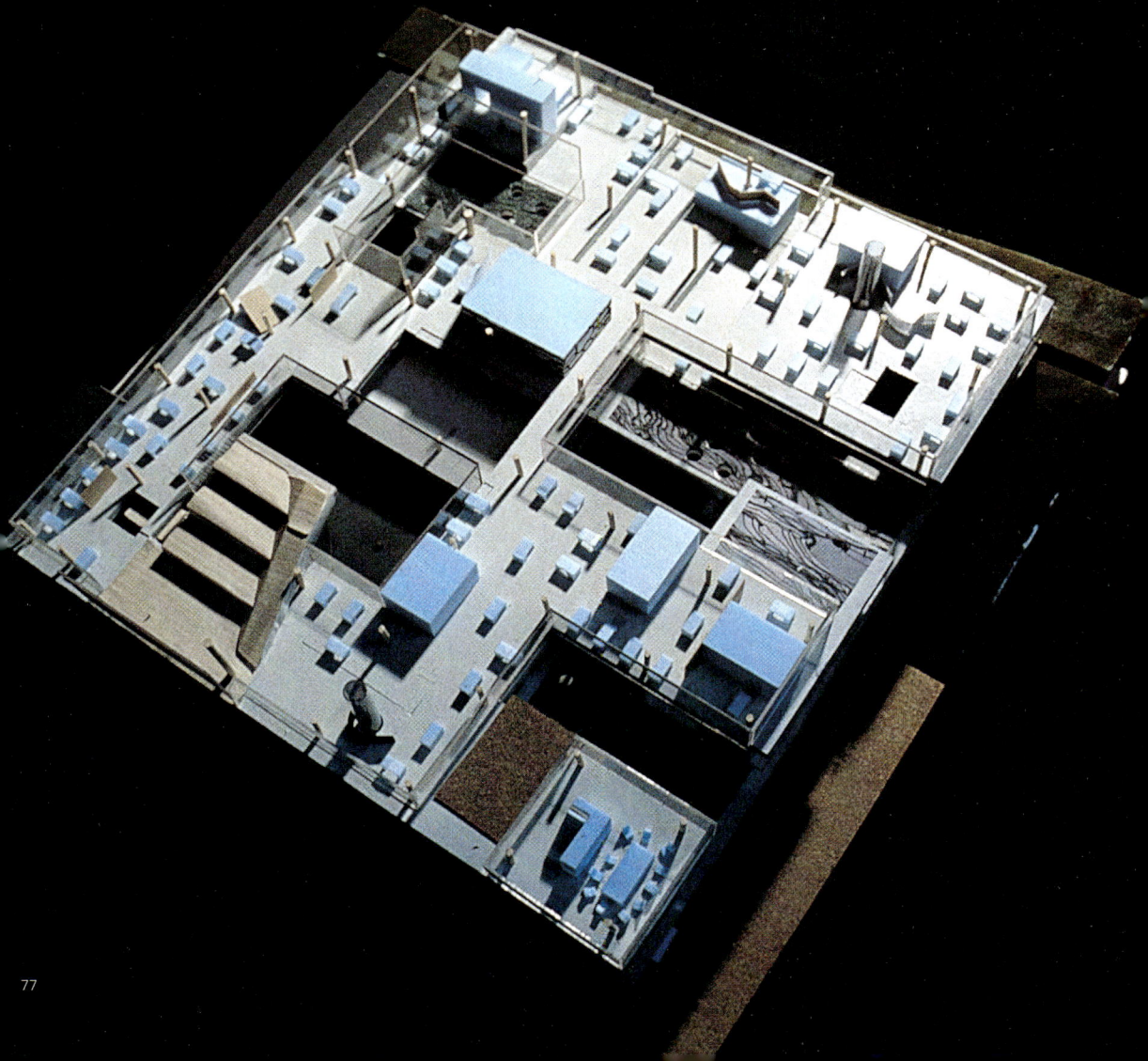

the office

Offices detail
1. general lighting
2. floorbox for electricity/data/telephone/tv
3. air outlet
4. sprinkler
5. cross bracing
6. construction floor
7. raised floor
8. column

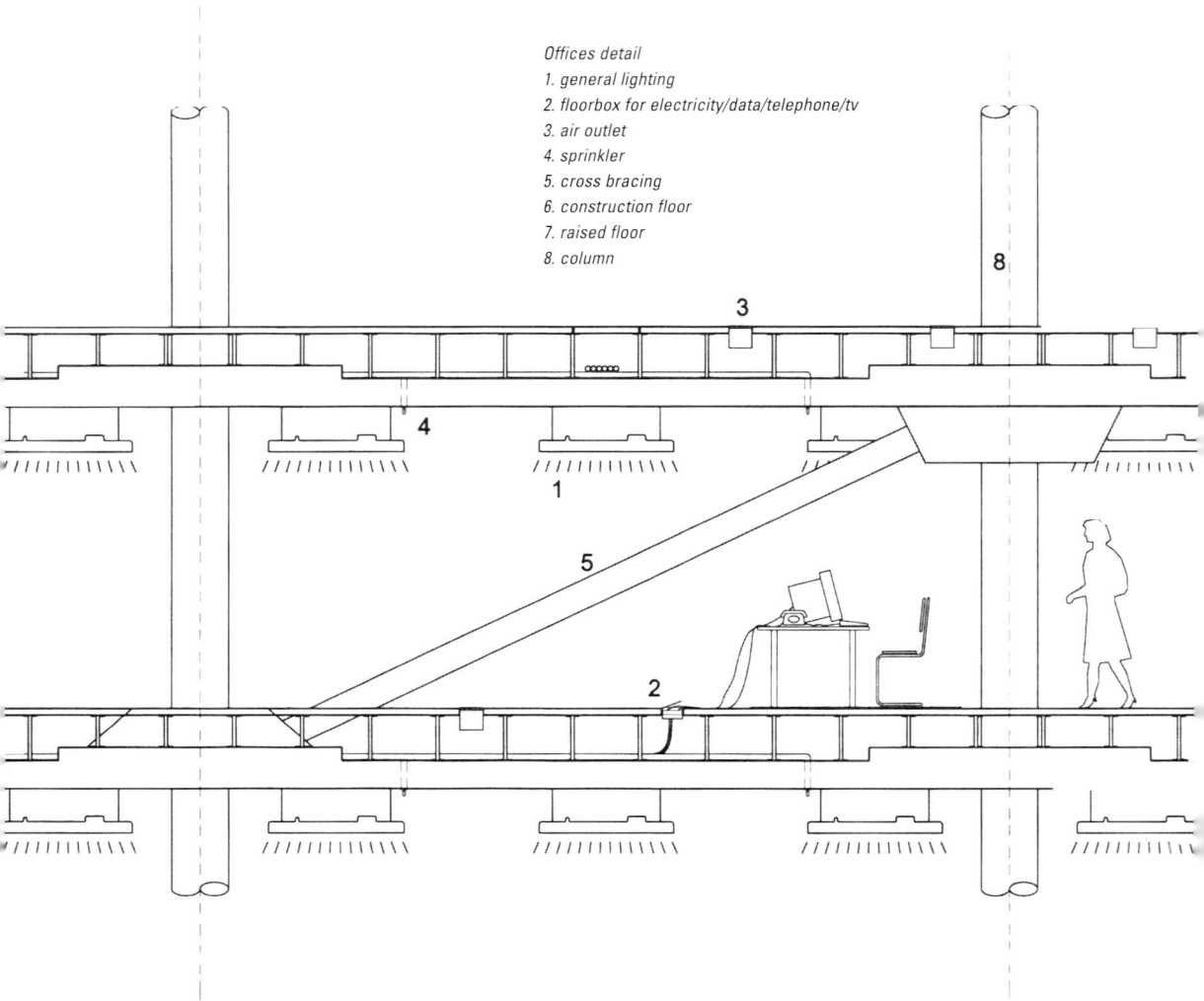

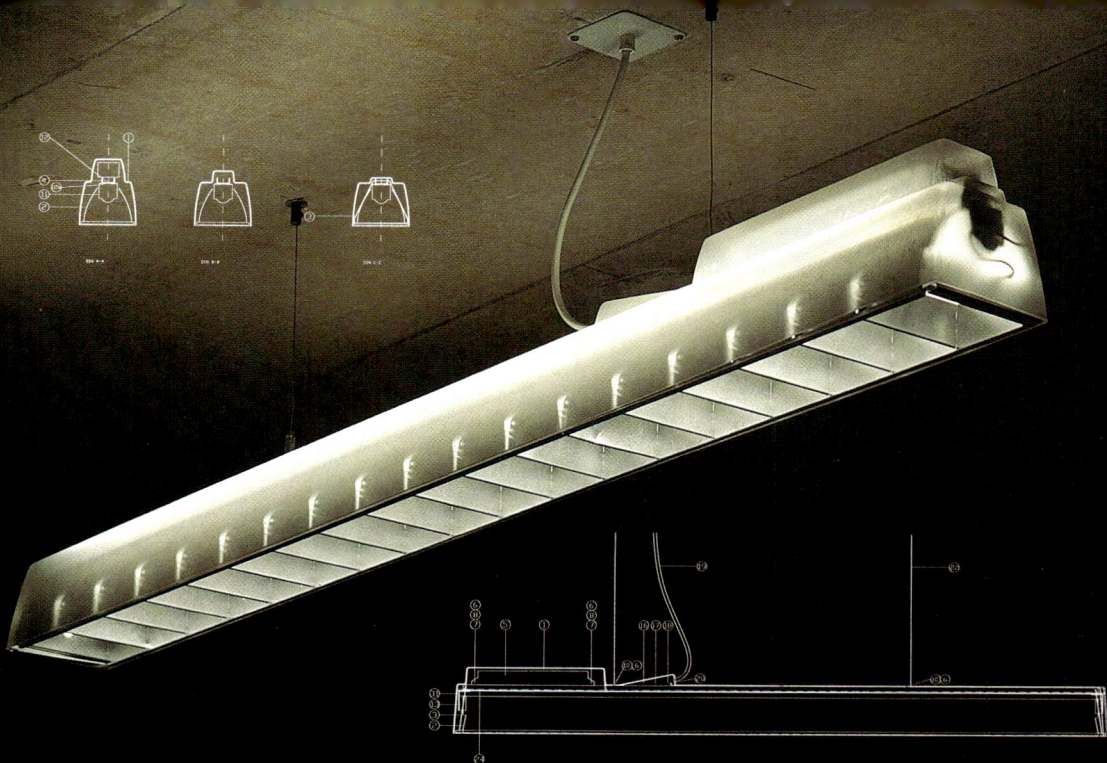

In these floors the technical facilities are hidden in an ancient Roman way. It's Spartan character serves as a commentary on the addictive aspects of present-day air-conditioning installations. They are fed with air, data and electricity through semi-transparent shafts.
The way the building has been materialized suggests the old villas; no lowered ceilings but a real ceiling, no prefabricated walls but stone, steel, wood and plastic.

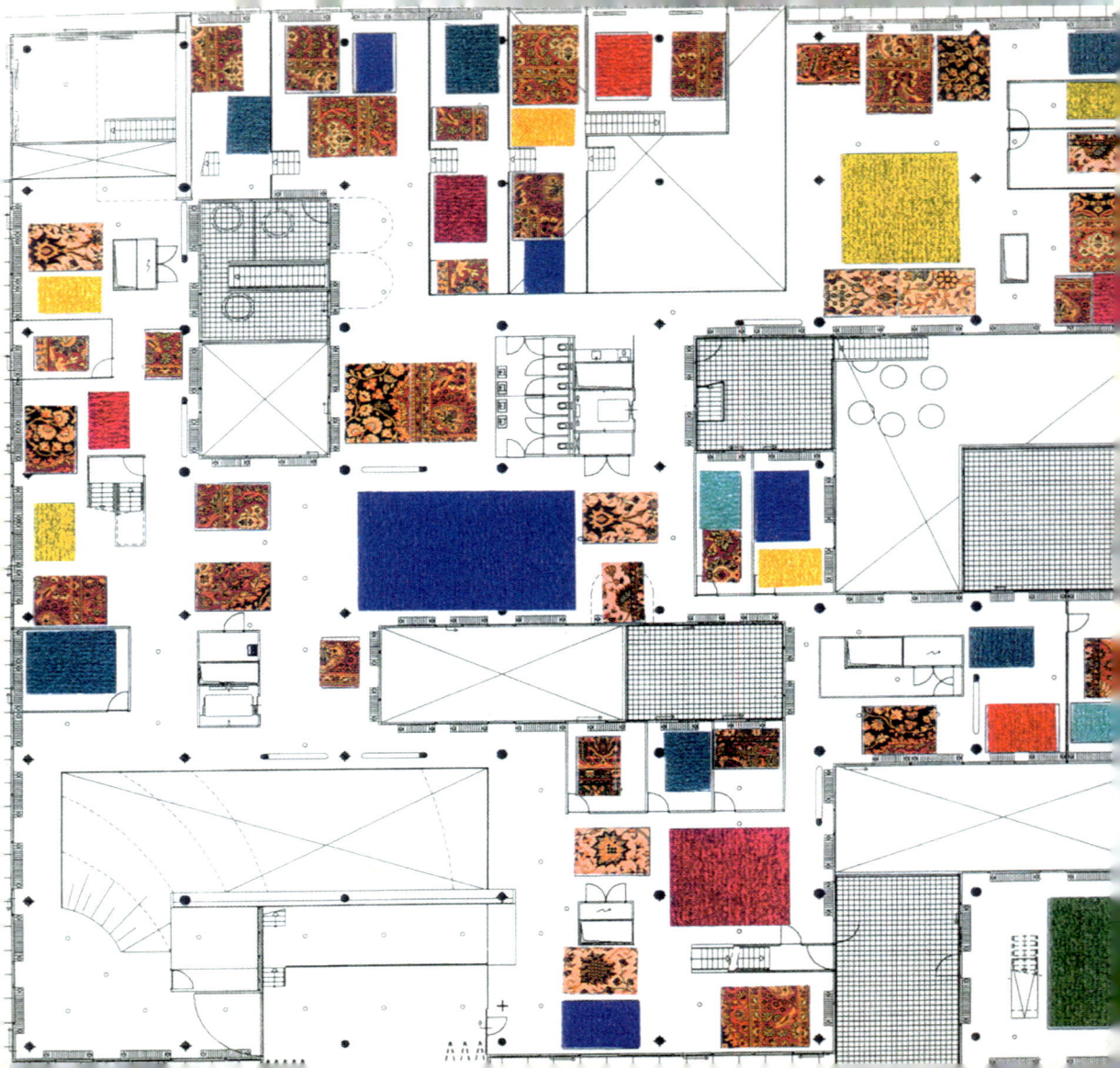

No project carpet but Persian and sisal rugs, no small windows but elevations containing storey-high sliding elements giving practically every office access to a garden, balcony, terrace or patio.
In the studios the standard fibre-cement panels are replaced by an arrangement of absorption and reflection using a wide variety of different materials such as wood, coconut fibre, fabric, steel and stone.

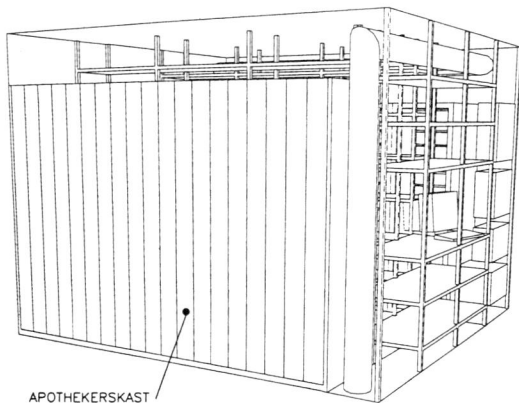

APOTHEKERSKAST

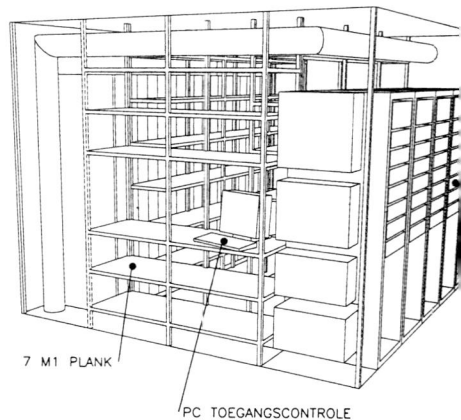

Reception box

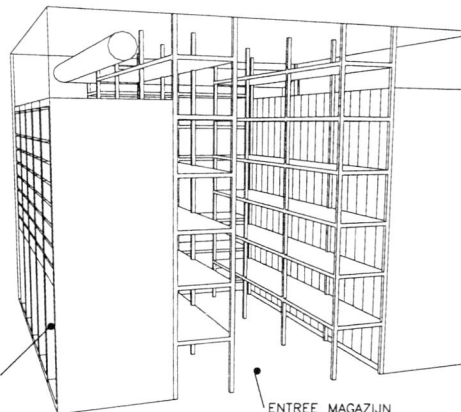

COPIEERKASTEN

ENTREE MAGAZIJN
AFSLUITBAAR

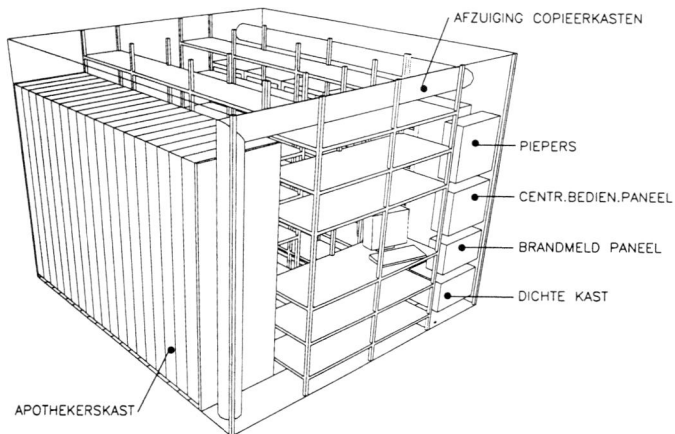

AFZUIGING COPIEERKASTEN

PIEPERS

CENTR.BEDIEN.PANEEL

BRANDMELD PANEEL

DICHTE KAST

APOTHEKERSKAST

7 M1 PLANK

PC TOEGANGSCONTROLE

SCHIJF MET 8 VAKKEN
SCHAAL 1:10

SCHIJF MET 6 VAKKEN
SCHAAL 1:10

BETONKOLOM/DIAMETER 500mm

BETONKOLOM DIAMETER 400mm

BERKENMULTIPLEX 18MM
BEPLAKT MET BERKEN FINEER
TRANSPARANT MAT GELAKT

GELEIDING ROND KOLOM
MET BEHULP VAN WIELTJES
ZOWEL ROND KOLOM Ø 400 ALS 500 mm

NAAD

8 VAKKEN

6 VAKKEN

6 VAKKEN

6 VAKKEN

8 VAKKEN

6 VAKKEN

8 VAKKEN

PLATTEGRONDEN

KAST OP WIELEN, MAX. 45 MM HOOG

KAST OP WIELEN, MAX. 45 MM HOOG

LINKS   RECHTS   VOOR   ACHTER
AANZICHTEN

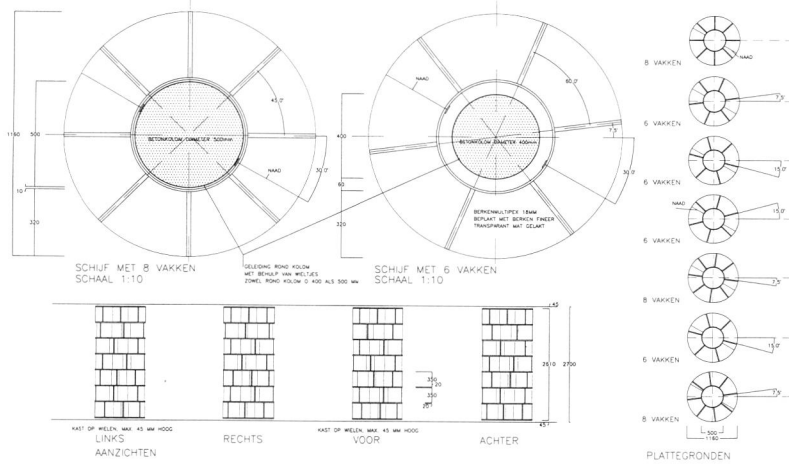

Revolving shelves around a column

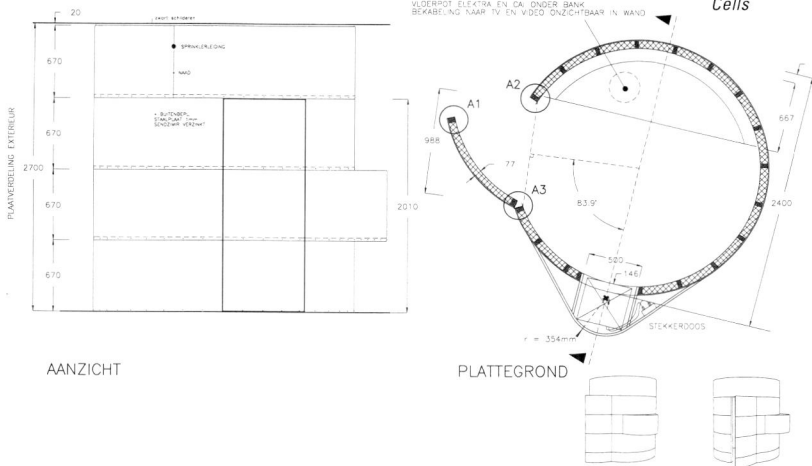

Cells

AANZICHT

PLATTEGROND

PLAATVERDELING EXTERIEUR

VLOERPOT ELEKTRA EN CAI ONDER BANK
BEKABELING NAAR TV EN VIDEO ONZICHTBAAR IN WAND

SPRINKLERLEIDING

NAAD

BUITENBPL.
STAALPLAAT 1 mm
GENDER? VERZINKT

A1   A2   A3

STEKKERDOOS

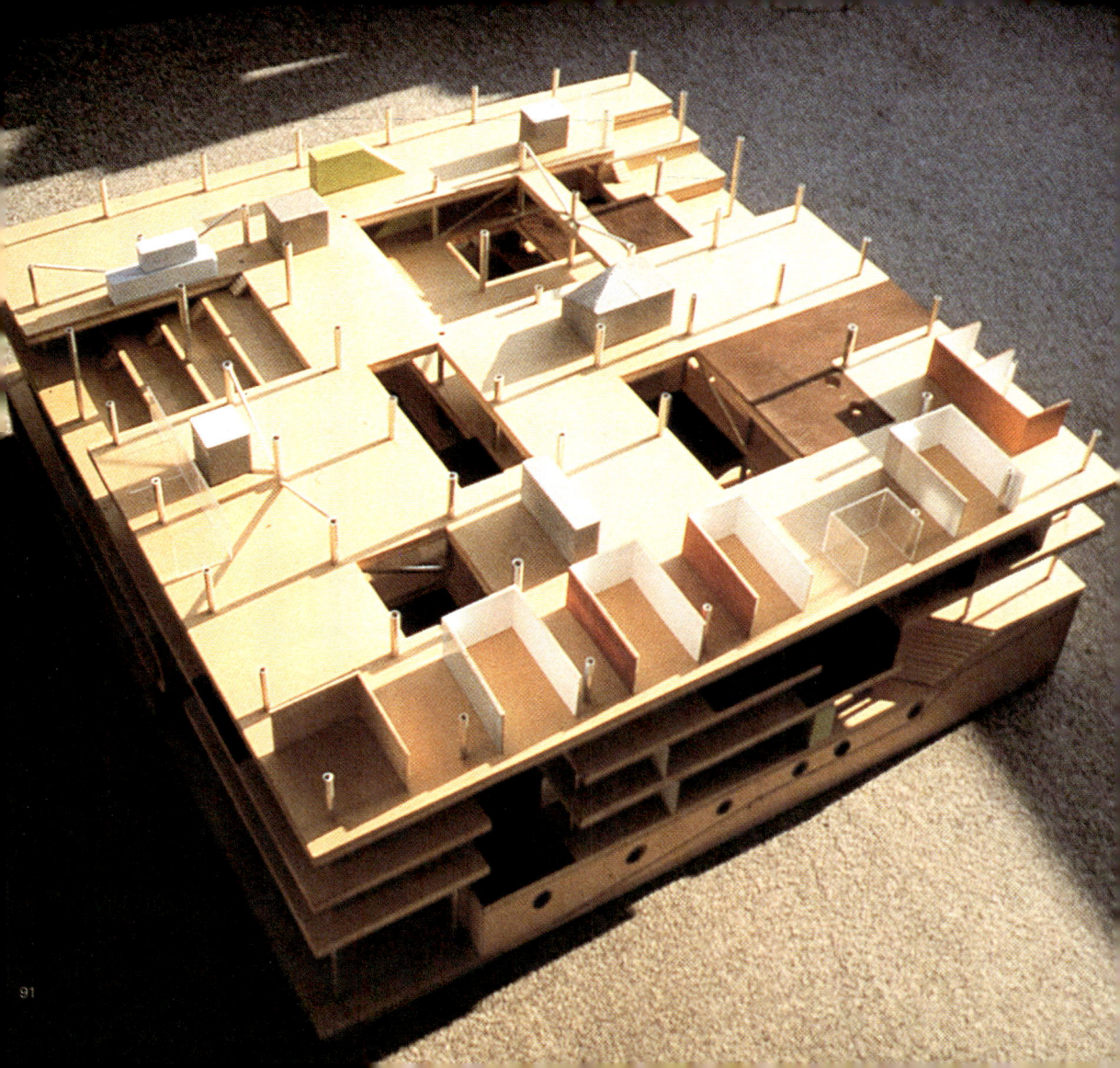

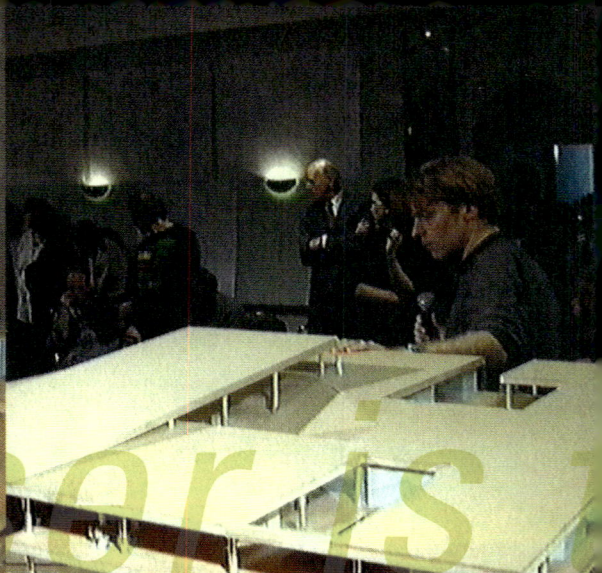

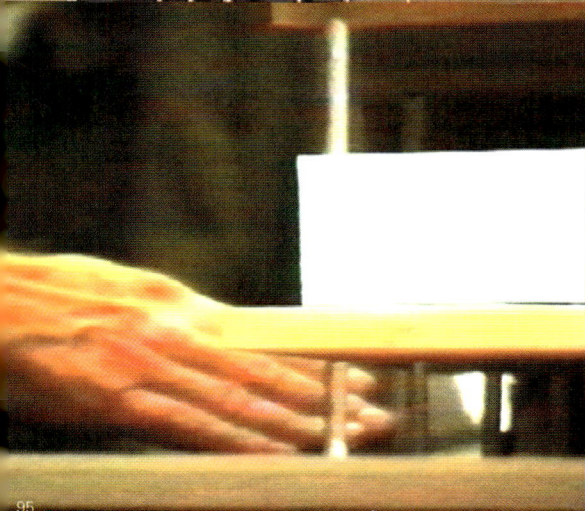

First presentation to the client. June / 1 / 1993
Comission. June / 22 / 1993
Initial siting analyses Program and office types. July / 7 / 1993 — **1**
Concept. Preliminary study 6 models. July / 13 / 1993 — **2**

Structural models. August / 24 / 1993 — **3**

Sketch of structure. September / 8 / 1993 — **4**

Sketch of structure. September / 17 / 1993 — **5**

Sketch of structure. September / 21 / 1993 — **6**

Approval of the new housing plans. November / 27 / 1993

Preliminary investigation. Schematic design phase

Plans and sections. January / 13 / 1994 — **1**
Proposals for internal organization. January / 13 / 1994 — **2**
I. Plan layout alternatives / II. Catalog / IIA. Loose elements
IIB. Fixed elements / IIC. Storage
4 expansion alternatives. January / 13 / 1994 — **3**

Elevations and sections. February / 3 / 1994 — **4**
Dark zones with and without views. February / 10 / 1994 — **5**
Spot plan. February / 10 / 1994 — **6**
Concept for interior partition layout alternatives — **7**
February / 10 / 1994
Package of floors - Elevations. February / 17 / 1994 — **8**

Plans / views. March / 3 / 1994 — **9**
Floor systems and elevation materials. March / 3 / 1994 — **10**
Plans – provisional sketches. March / 10 / 1994 — **11**
Acoustics in the offices. March / 17 / 1994 — **12**
Elevation study. March / 17 / 1994 — **13**
Area calculations. March / 31 / 1994 — **14**

Proposal of a new solution for the parking & — **15**
grid plans 7.2 m + areas. April / 20 / 1994

Study-example of flexibility. May / 24 / 1994 — **16**

Definitive design phase Grid study. June / 2 / 1994 — **1**

Construction documents

2 — August / 1 / 1995. Network influences 3

3 — October / 30 / 1995. Alternative layouts for studio

4 — February / 6 / 1996. Color palette

5 — April / 10 / 1996. Entrance area

6 — April / 10 / 1996. Green roof

7 — Novembre / 19 / 1996. Painting of parking platform

8 — December / 5 / 1996. Finishes

1996

Concept-DO for the elevations. July / 7 / 1994 — **3**

Design development phase
Restaurant organization. November / 9 / 1994 — **1**

Revisions. January / 9 / 1995 — **2**

Proposals for the building interior. January / 24 / 1995 — **3**

Proposals for the building interior. February / 9 / 1995 — **4**
Proposals for the building interior. February / 16 / 1995 — **5**
Proposals for the glass types. February / 22 / 1995 — **6**
Area reserved for window washing — **7**
Interior revision. February / 22 / 1995 — **8**
Location of sun shading in the elevation. February / 22 / 1995 — **9**

Acoustic proposals. April / 13 / 1995 — **10**
Synthetic products chart. April / 13 / 1995 — **11**
Revision core 3 level 2. April / 13 / 1995 — **12**
Sudy of balcony size. April / 14 / 1995 — **13**

Focal points in the design development — **14**
May / 4 / 1995

Illumination. May / 30 / 1995 — **15**

Construction documents
Public area mechanical services. June / 29 / 1995 — **1**

9 — May / 14 / 1997. Toilet room fixtures

Removal. May / 29 / 1997

First day of work. June / 2 / 1997

Opening party. August / 29 / 1997

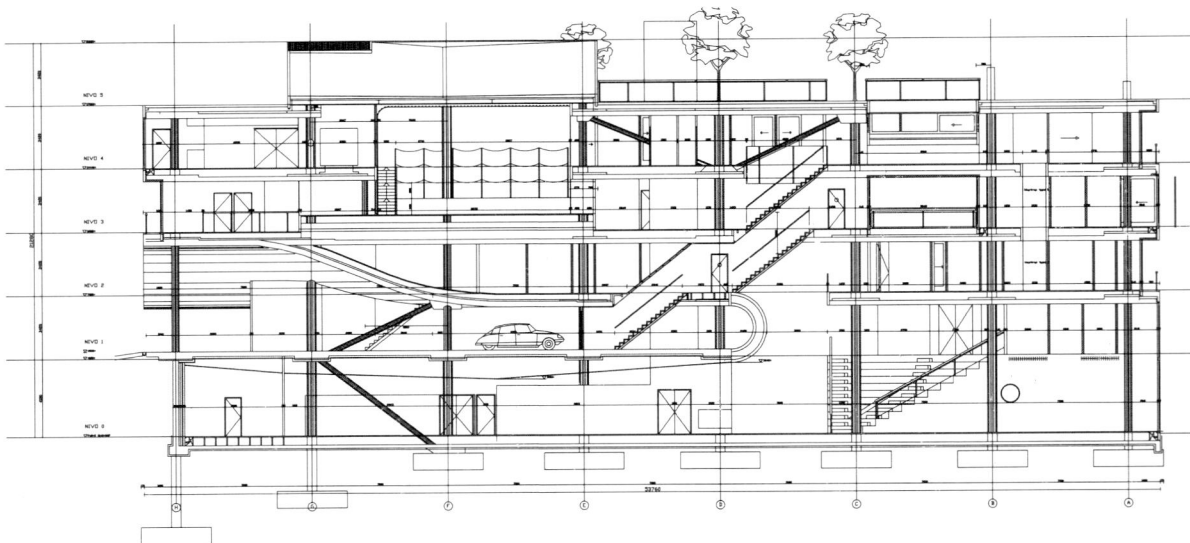

Compactness, the absence of long corridors, spatial differentiation, a large number of different rooms, and a close relationship to the landscape around it are the key terms to describe the villa.

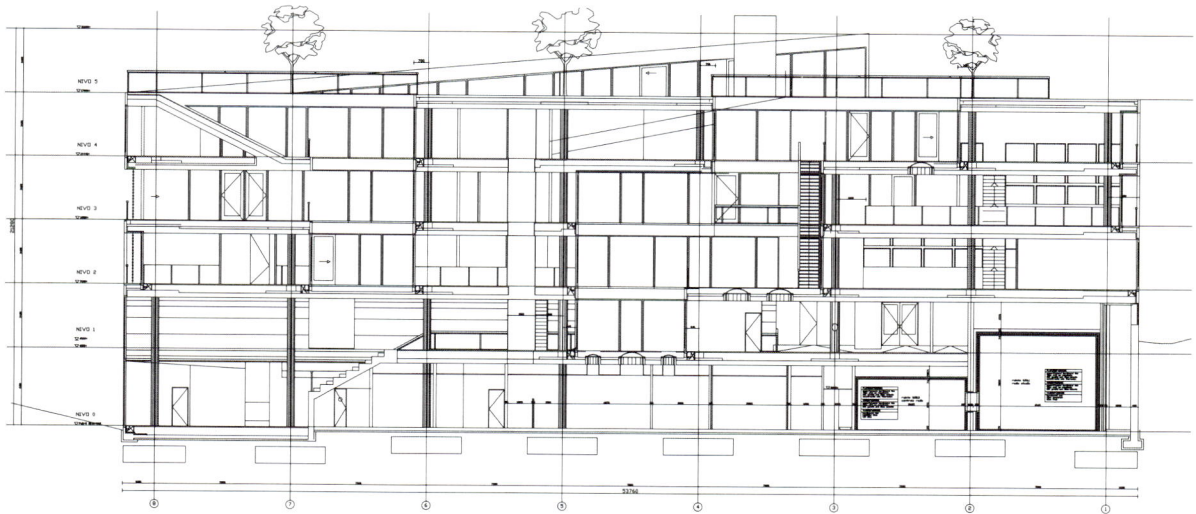

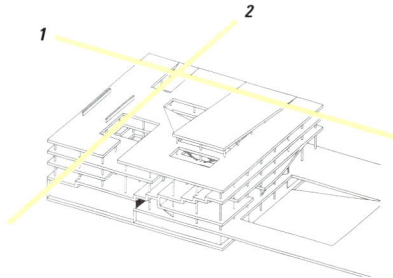

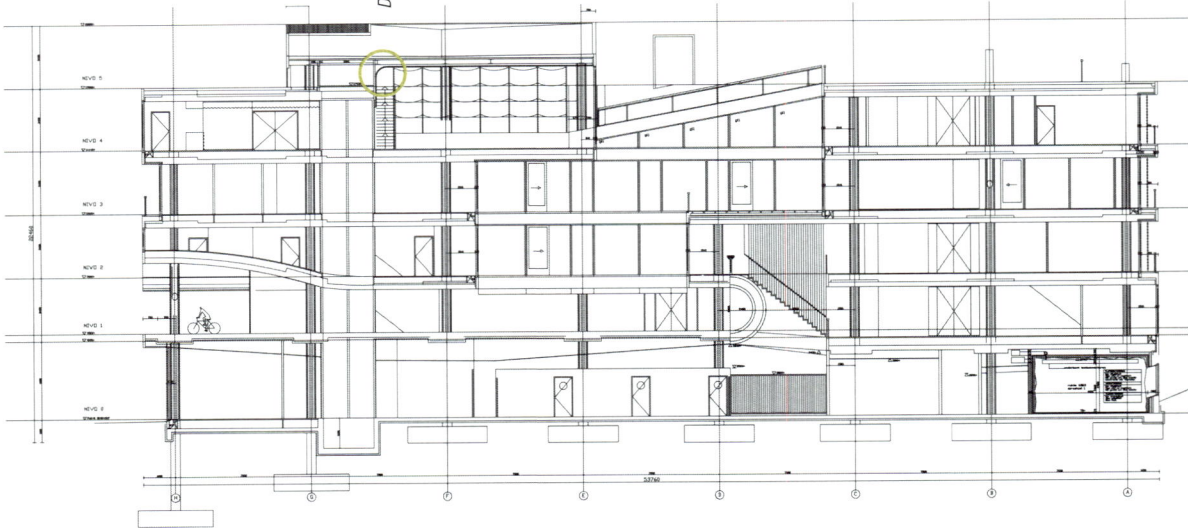

The differences in height in the resulting continuous interior, combined with the wings created by the gaps, have provided the possibillity to position a wide range of work contexts in different office typologies.

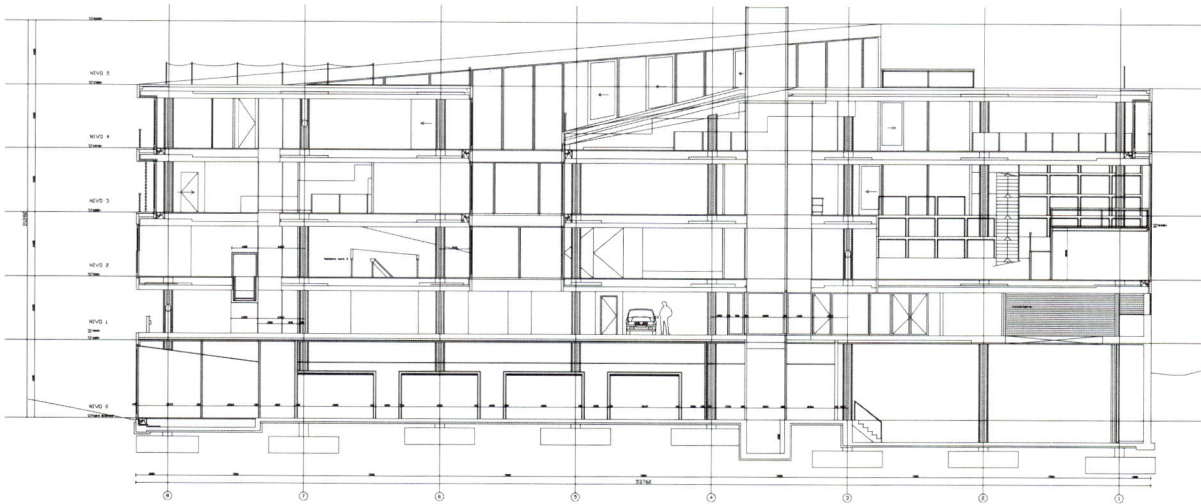

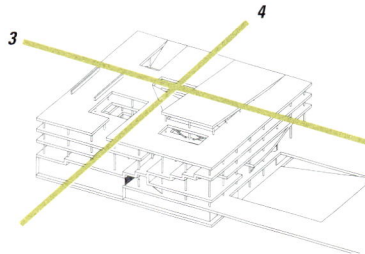

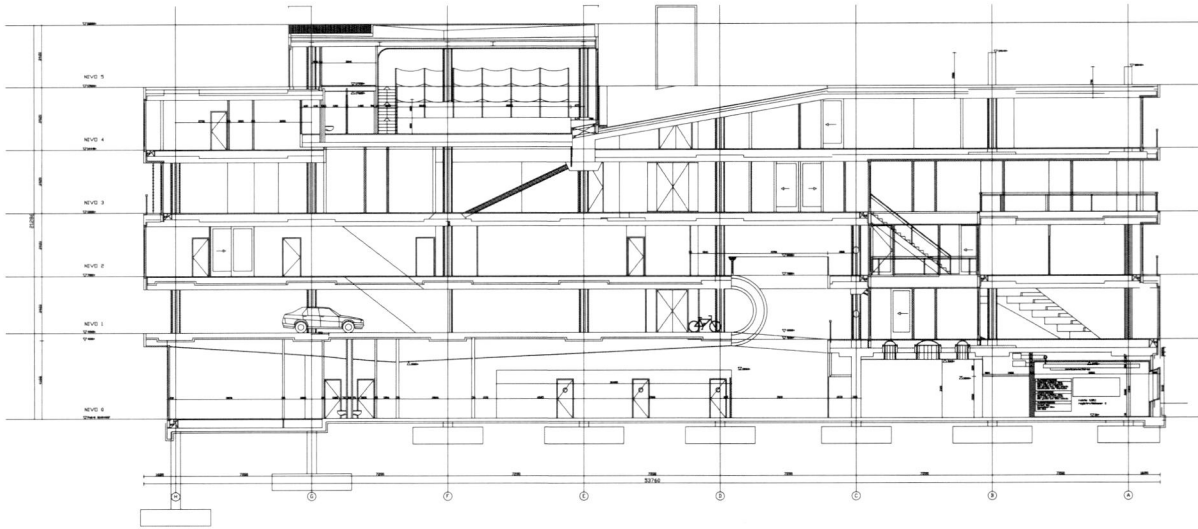

The combination of the ever changing groups of radio and tv-programm makers and more permanent general staff of the VPRO organisation demanded this hybrid solution.

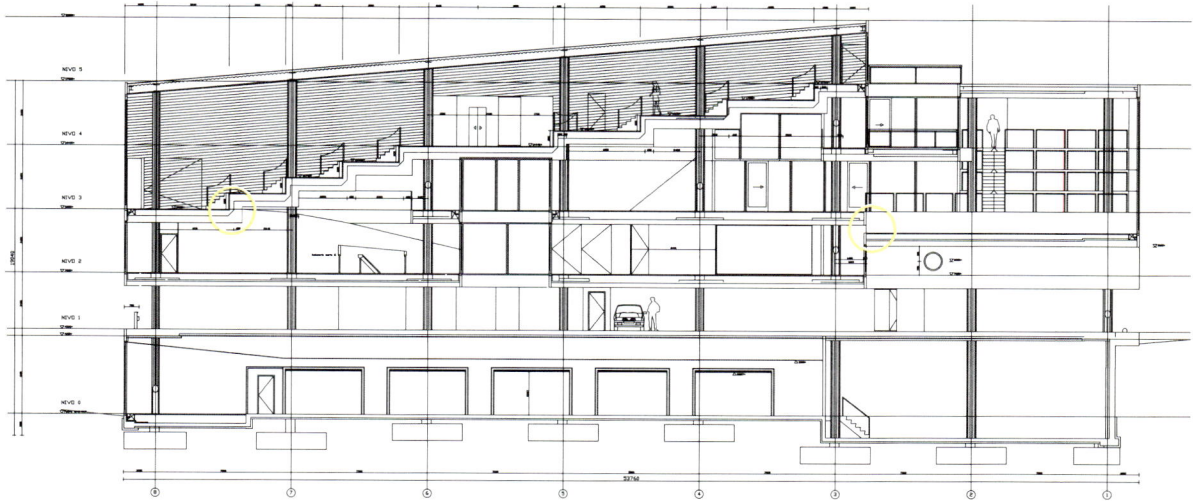

Detail page 108

Detail page 109

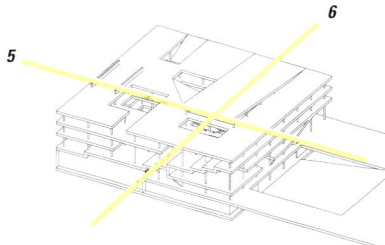

Detail page 109

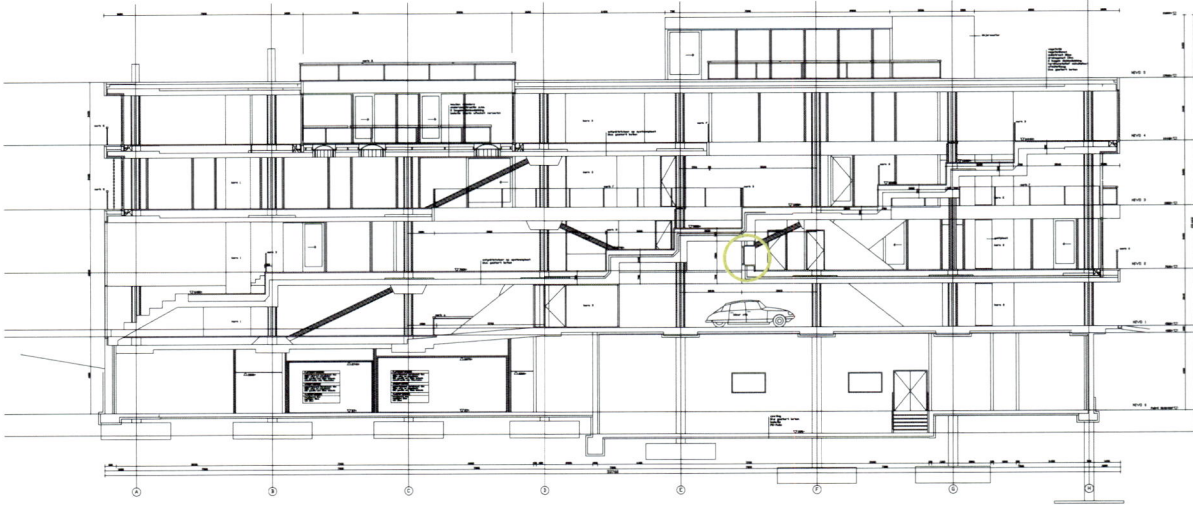

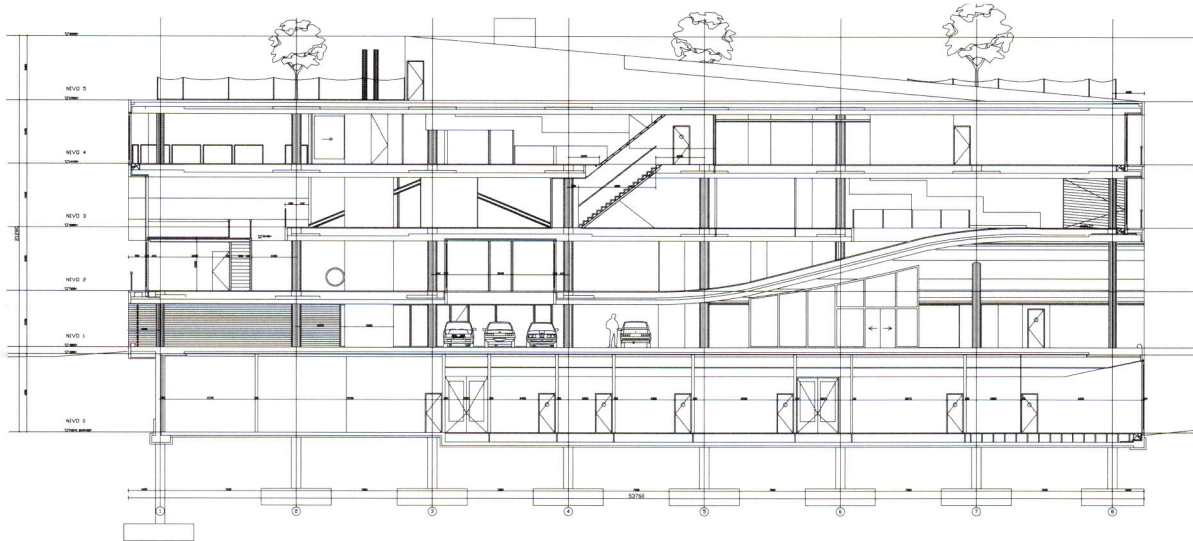

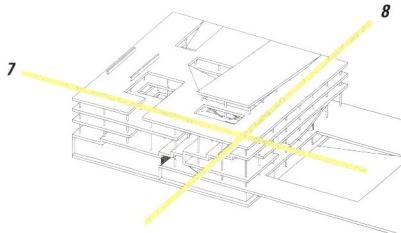

Restaurant details

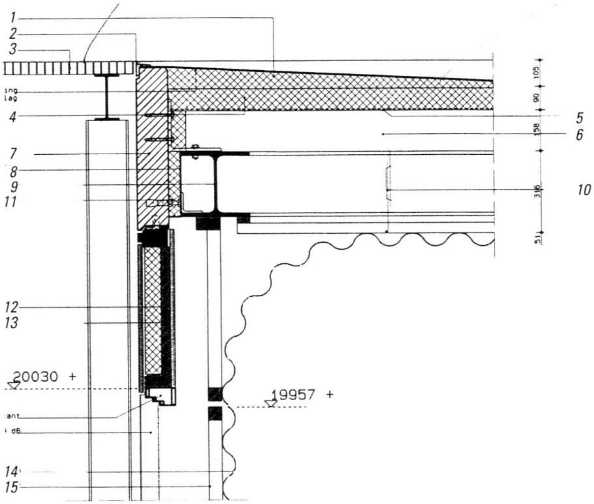

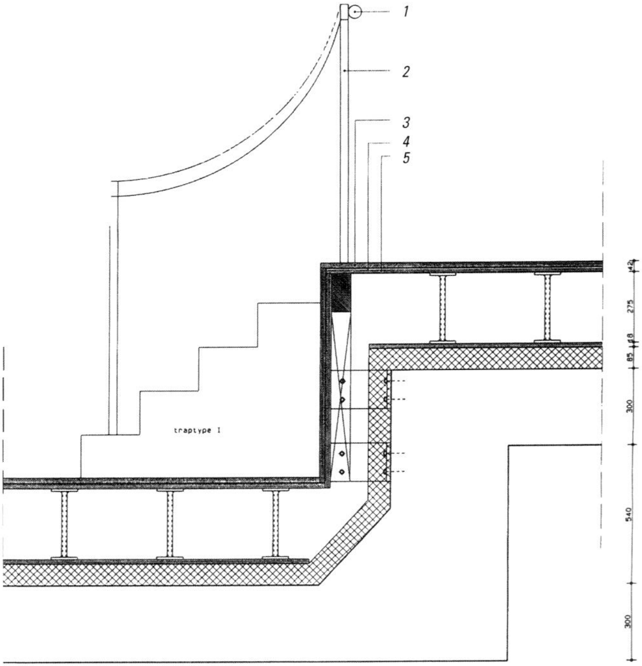

Floor:
1. rings to attach rope 50 mm
2. balustrade
3. parkett floor 20 mm
4. foam
5. underlayment 19 mm

Roof:
1. roof cladding
2. metal angle
3. grill roof 30 x 30 x 50 mm
4. foamboard
5. steamproof membrane
6. steel roofsheets h=158 mm d=1,4 mm
7. prefab concrete
8. membrane
9. HE260A
10. construction ceiling
11. adjustable bolt
12. steamproof membrane
13. isolation
14. corrugated plastic sheet 171 x 51 mm
15. wooden construction

Level 2:

1. in situ concrete
2. Glaswool isolation
3. prefab polyester concrete
4. anhydrite floor
5. plenum
6. cocoon
7. triplex
8. foamboard isolation
9. Glaswool isolation

Window below terraced hall at level 2:

1. silicon joint
2. in situ concrete
3. foamboard isolation
4. wooden construction
5. prefab polyester concrete

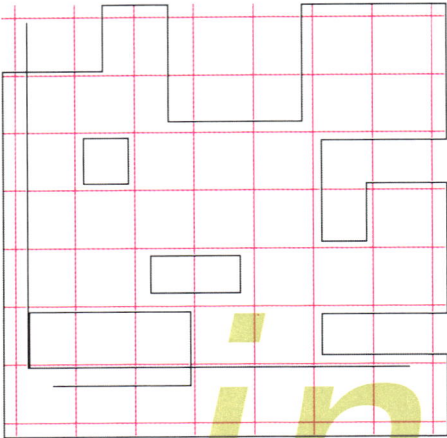

Grid

Voids

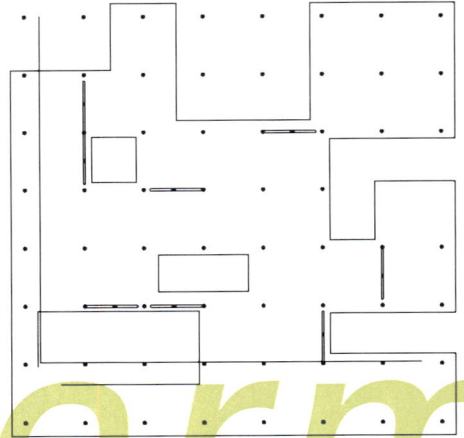

Structure

Daylight

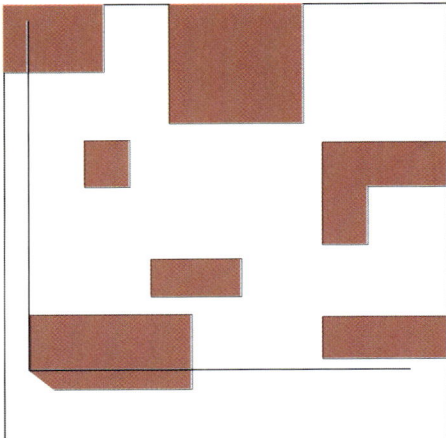

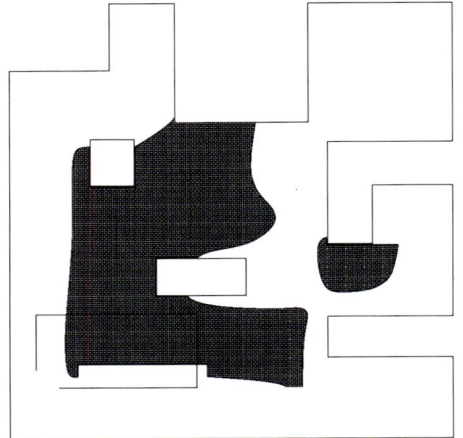

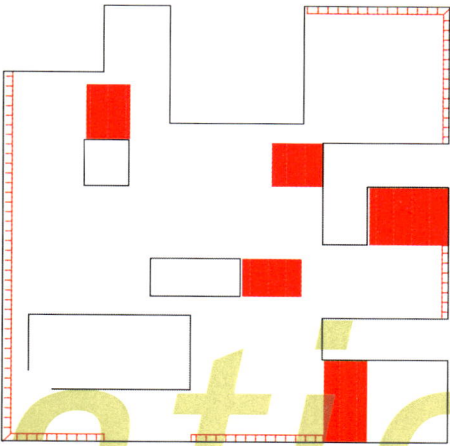

Terraces

Stairs

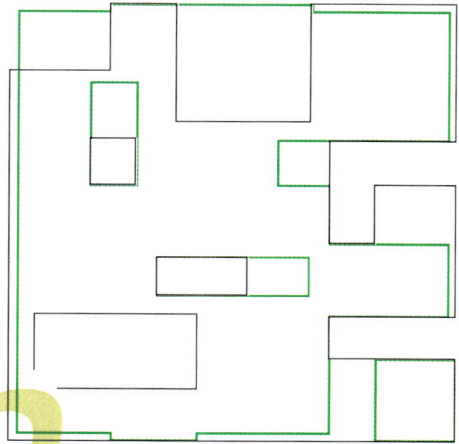

Facades

Emergency routes

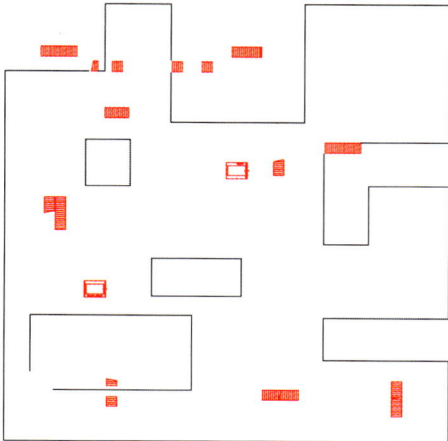

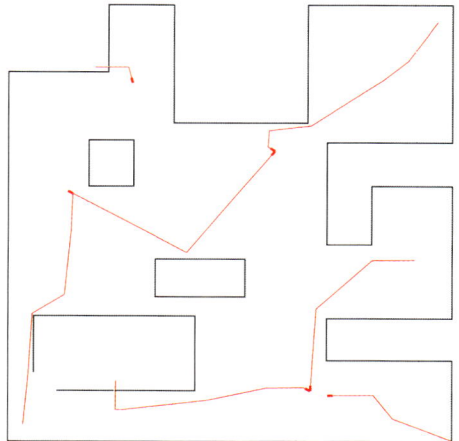

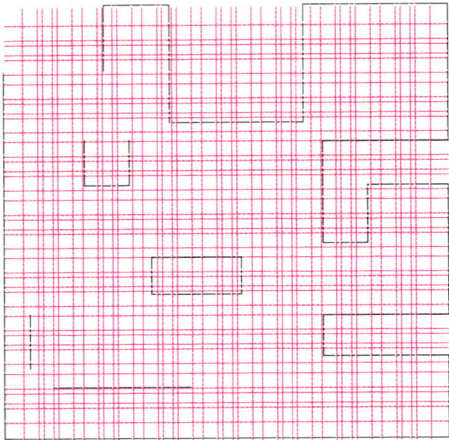

Facilities

Data

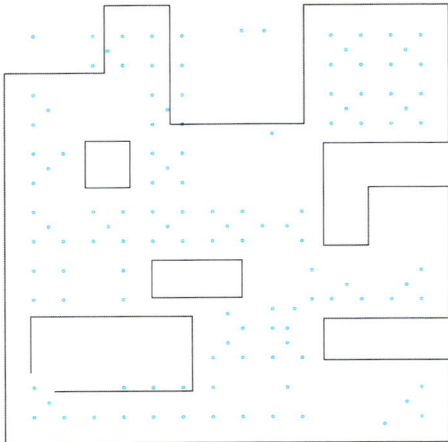

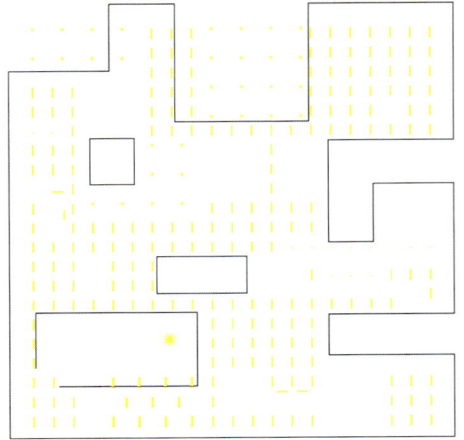

Lighting

Air conditioning and heating

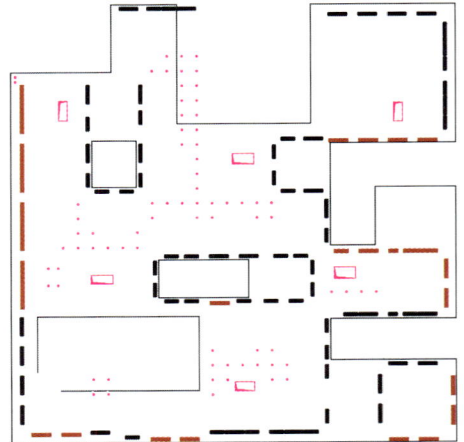

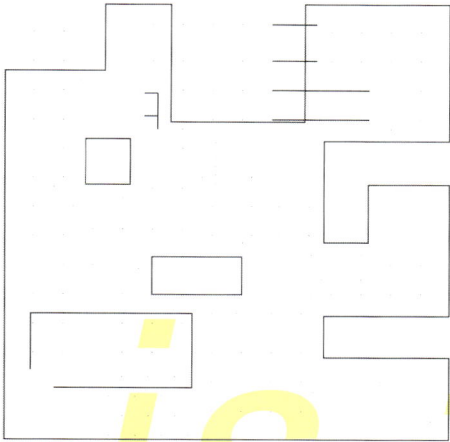
Sprinklers

Rugs

Partitions

Superposition

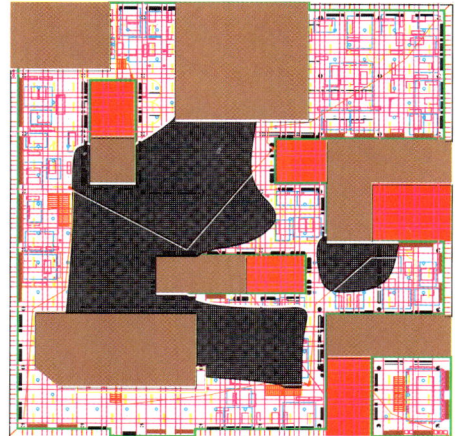

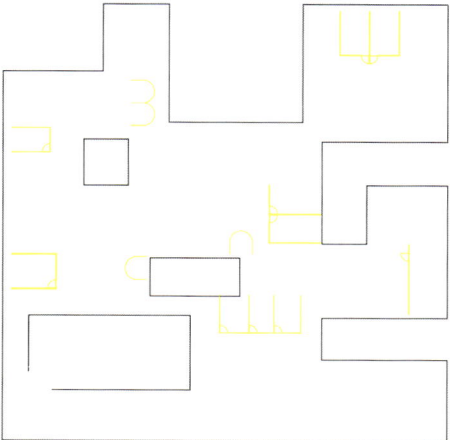

is form

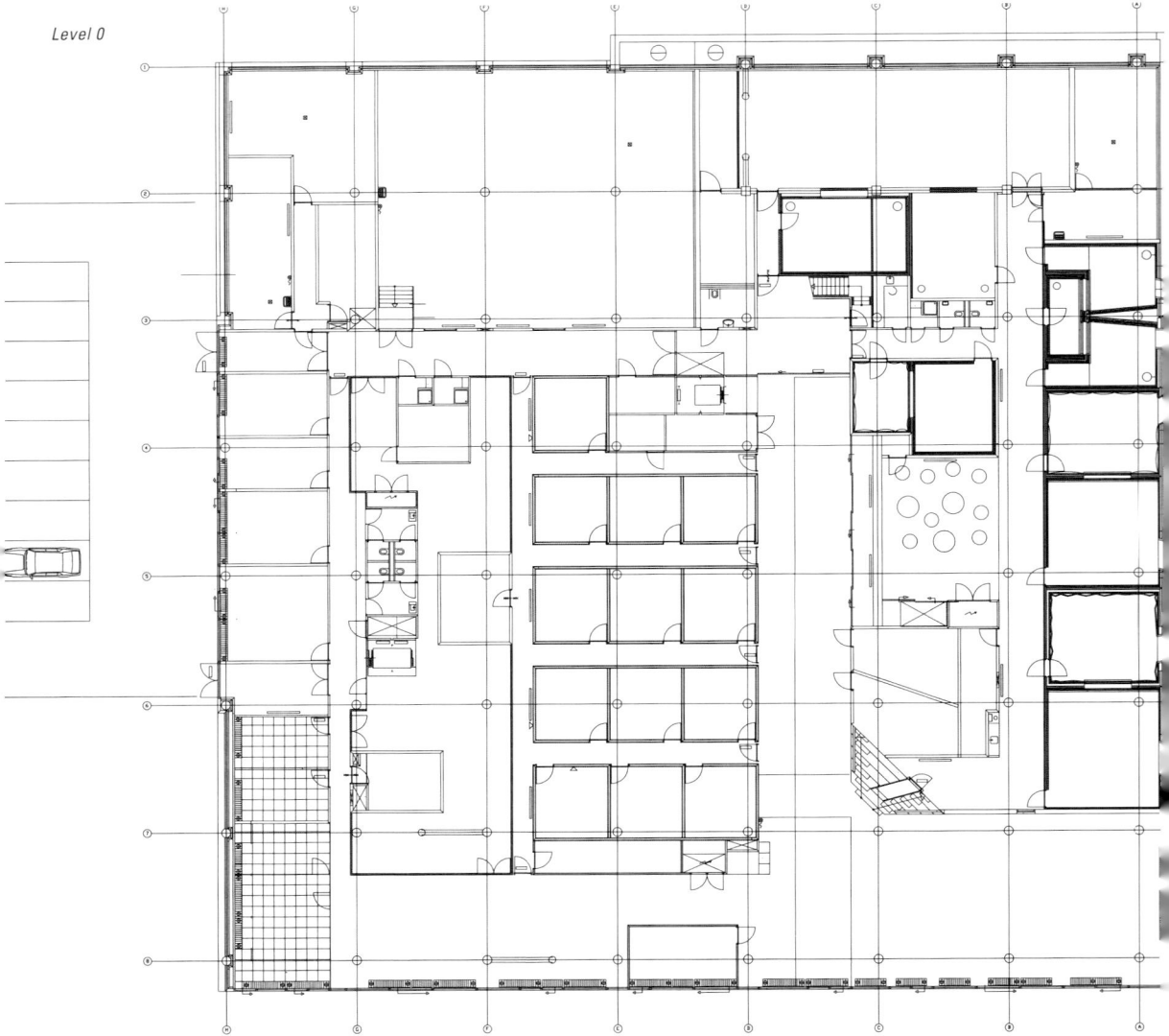

Level 0

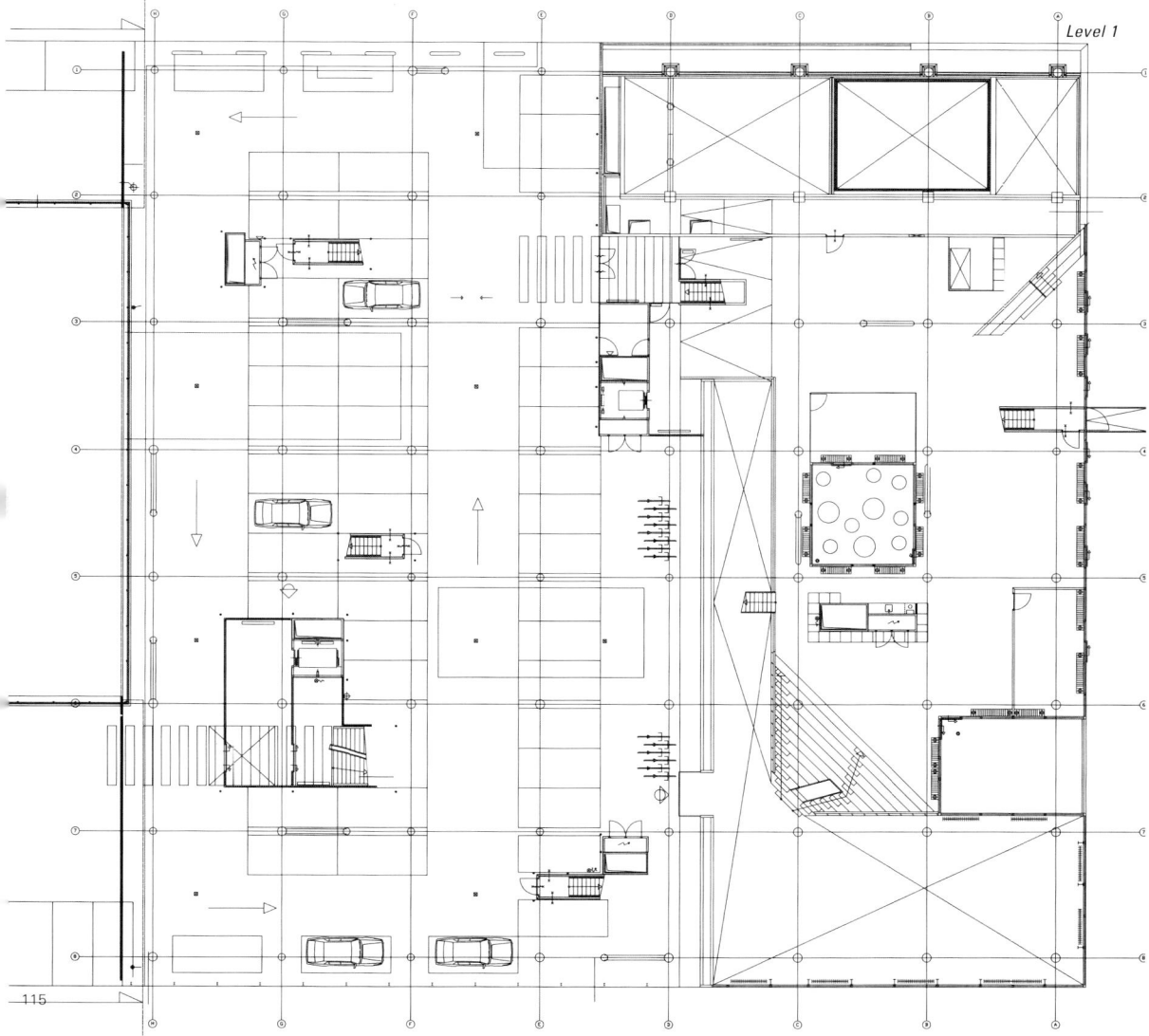

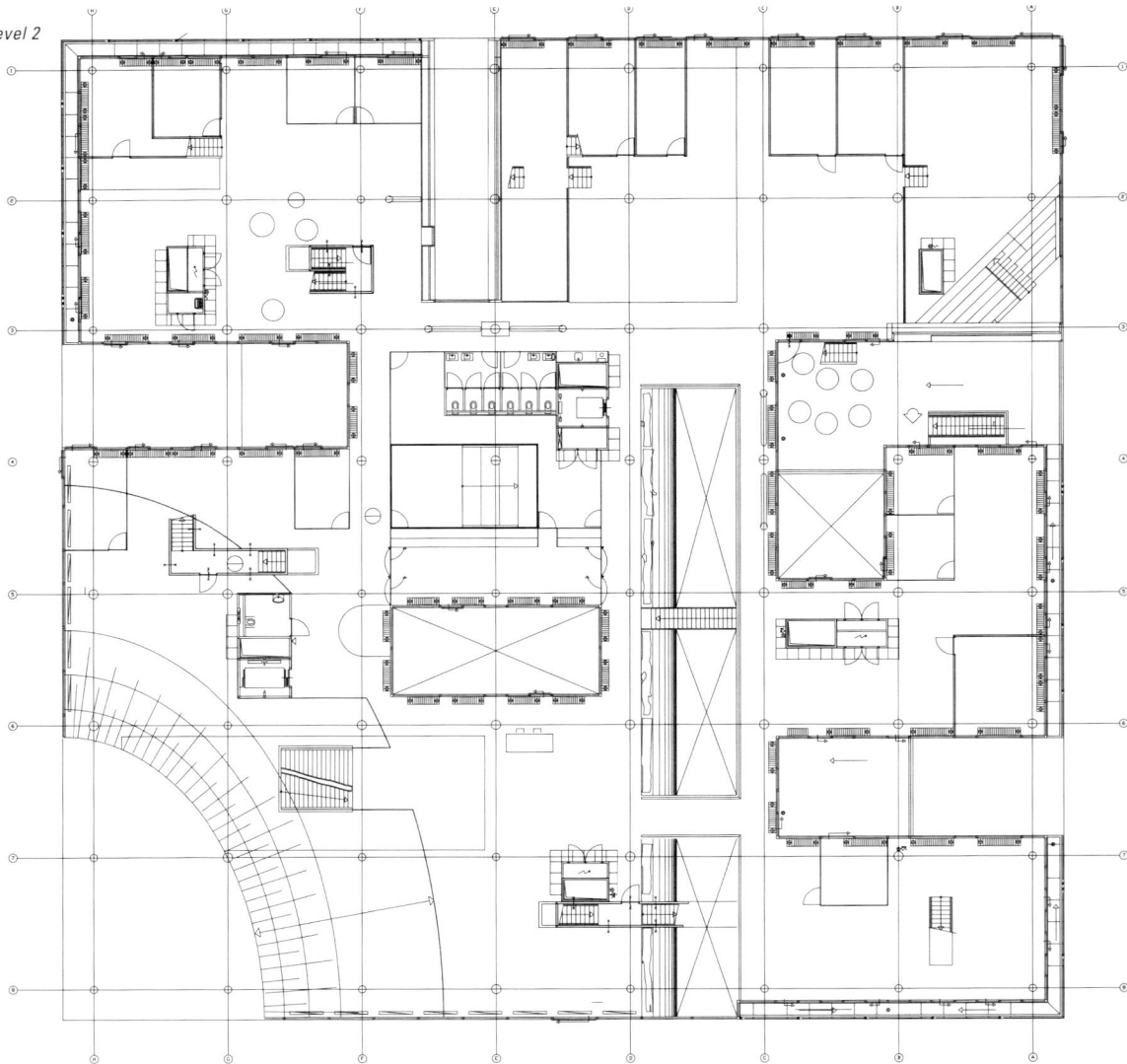

Level 2

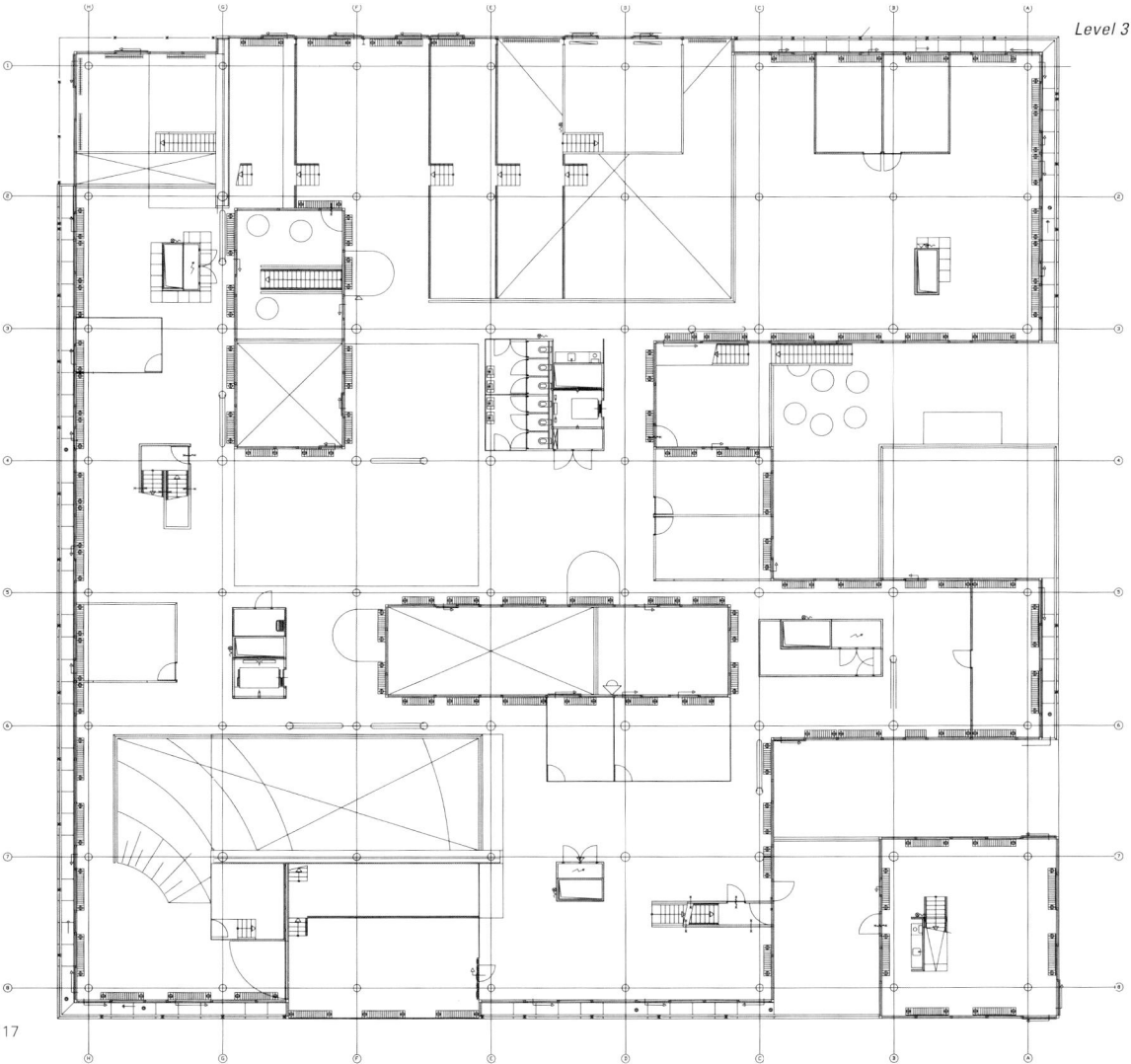

117

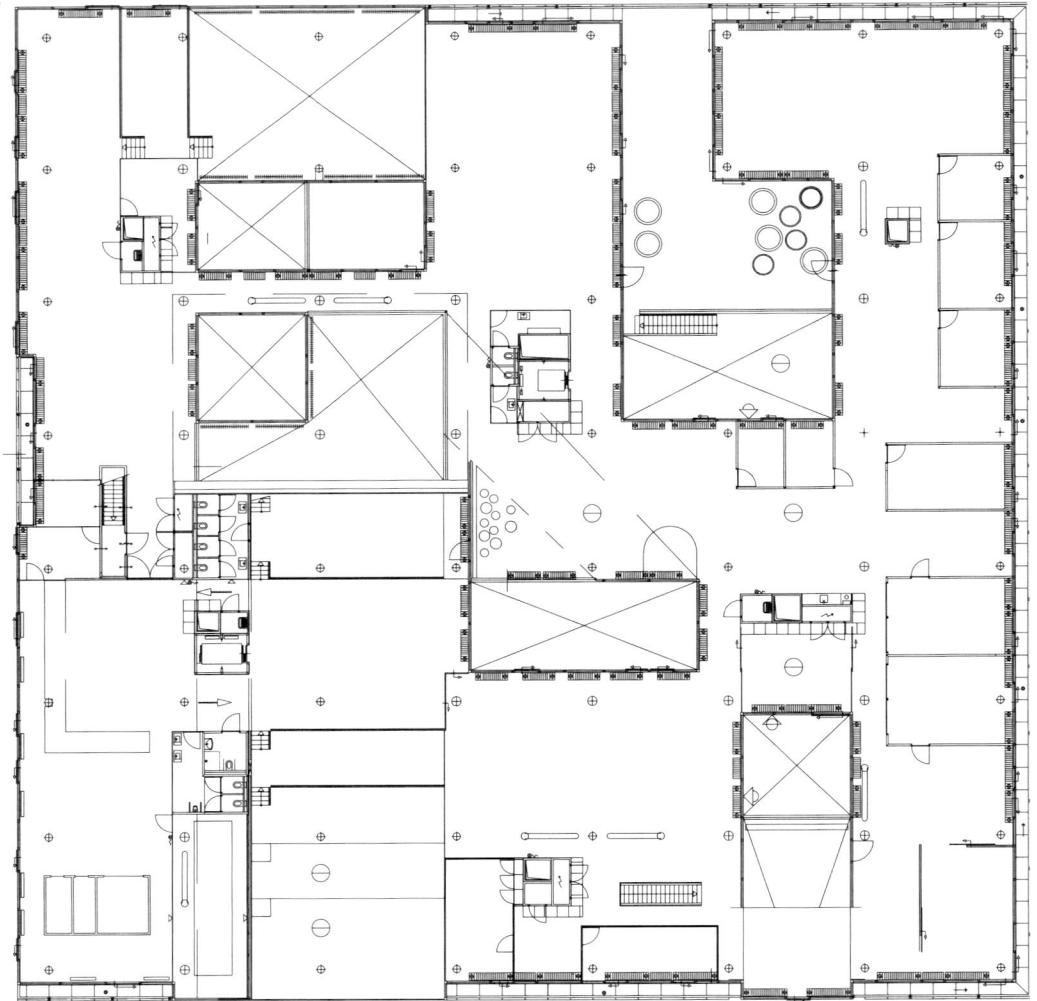

119

the floor is

the facade

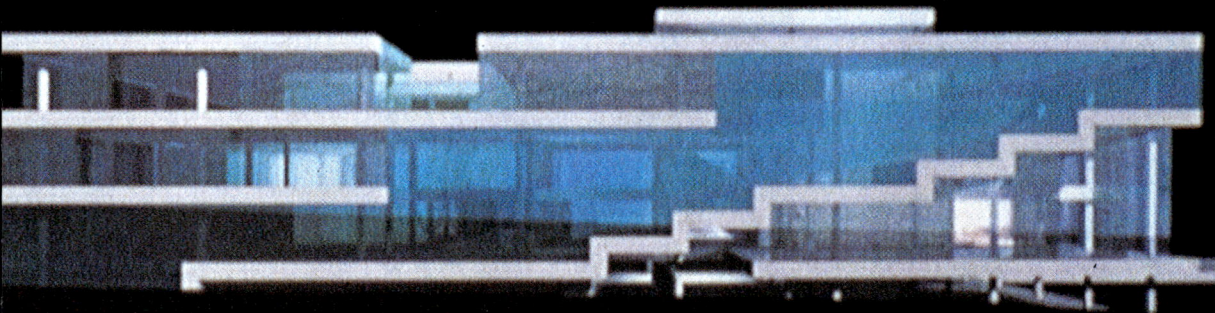

East elevation

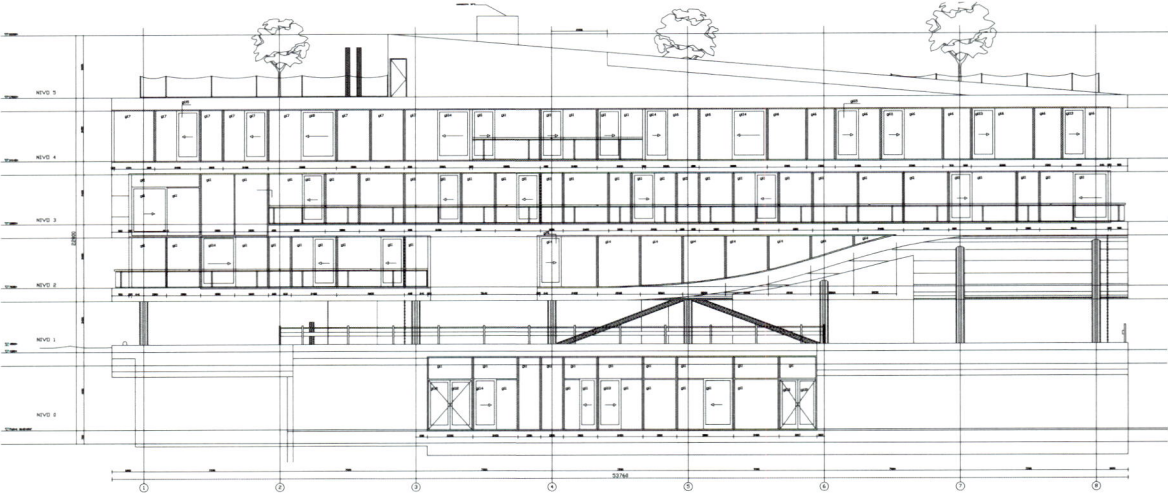

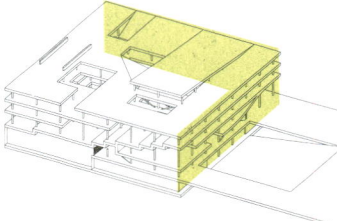

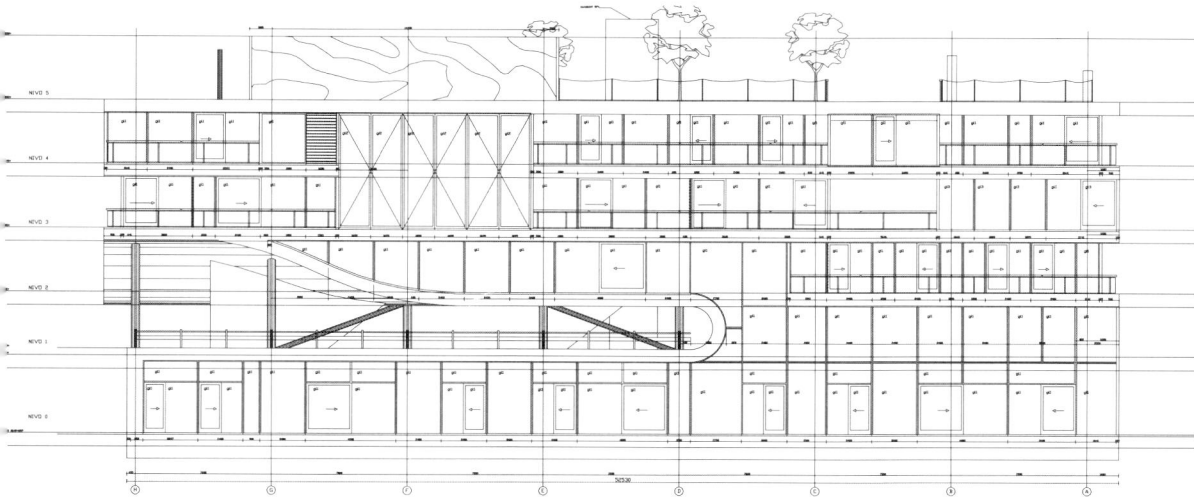

The frontage is the outcome of a datascape of requirements. To provide the most generous outlook possible over the attractive surroundings, the original proposal was for a frontage made up of a system of hot-air blowers.

West elevation

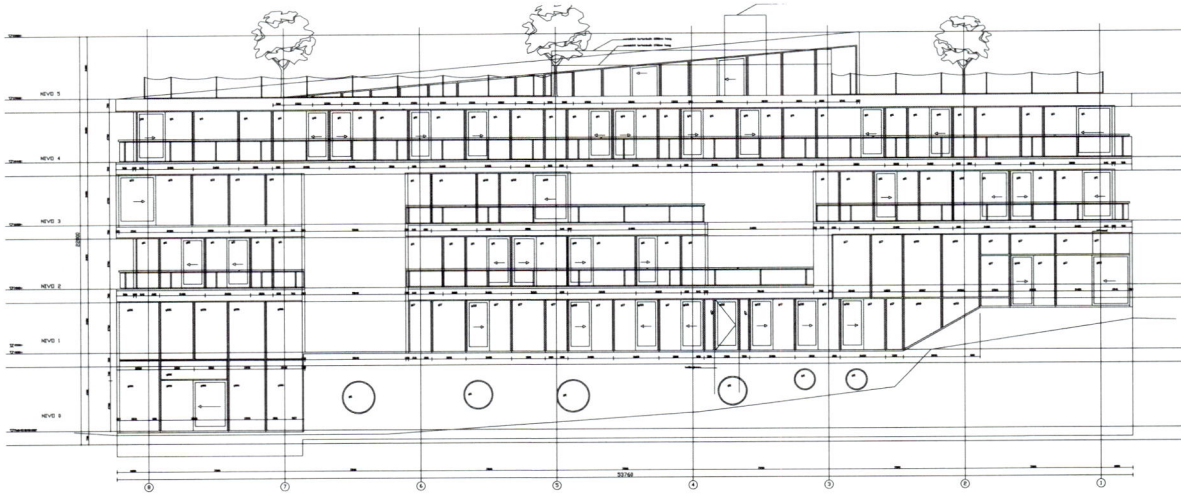

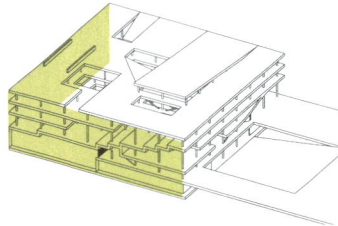

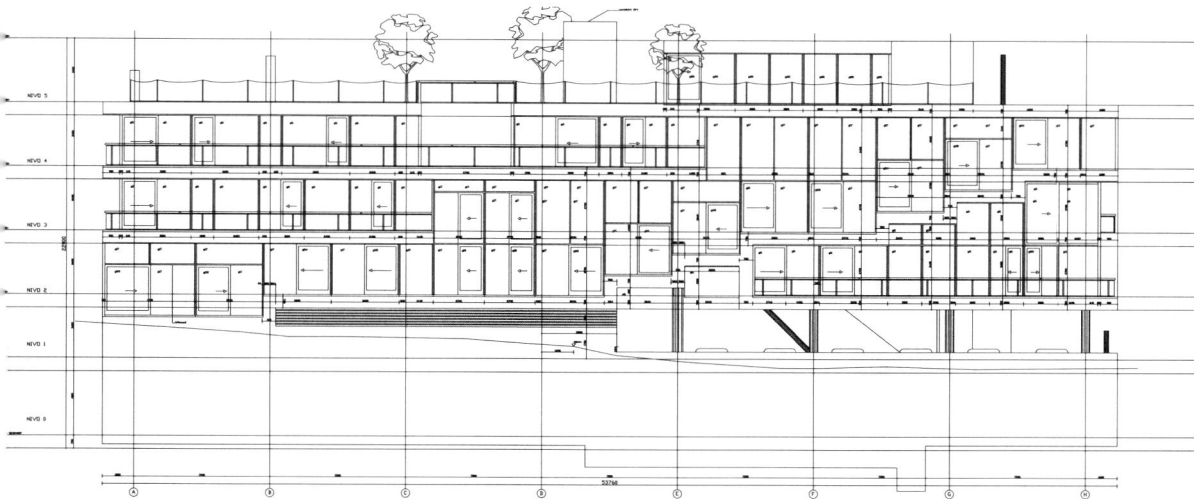

But since such an arrangement was not legally permissible, the idea was replaced by one using 35 different sorts of glass, whose colour, reflectivity, and degree of transparency reflect the different ways they are positioned relative to the rooms lying behind them.

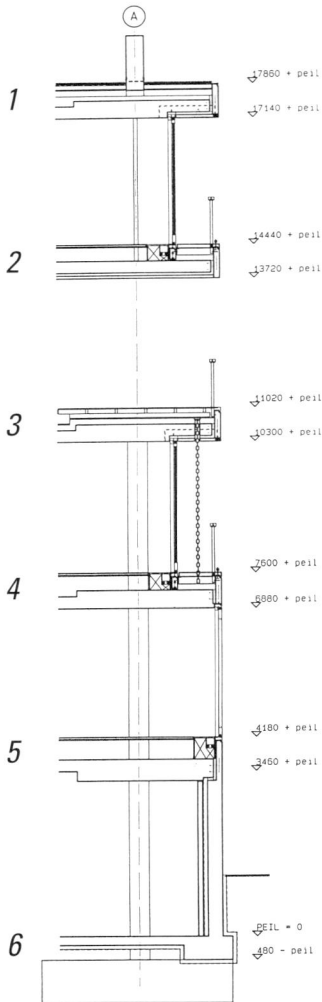

Ⓐ

1

17860 + peil
17140 + peil

2

4440 + peil
3720 + peil

3

1020 + peil
10300 + peil

4

7600 + peil
6880 + peil

5

4180 + peil
3460 + peil

6

PEIL = 0
480 - peil

1
1. grass
2. grass mat
3. 80 mm substrate
4. 17 mm drainage mat
5. two layers roofing membrane
6. synthetic foam insulation board
7. leveling slab
8. concrete floor slab
9. stainless steel anchor
10. 60 mm synthetic foam insulation board
11. poured-in-place concrete slab
12. metal roof trim
13. lead
14. prefabricated concrete edge panel
15. embedded anchor to support sunscreens
16. upper rail of moveable sunscreen
    (with electric controls at east elevation)

2
1. hardwood rail
2. steel T 80 x 40 x 5 mm
3. prefabricated concrete floor tile
4. 30mm diameter holes at 100 mm O.C.
5. rubber sheet
6. rubber sheet
7. water drainage channel
8. two layers roofing membrane
9. synthetic foam insulation board (with integrated slope)
10. synthetic raised flooring
11. wooden grating with metal angle frame
12. vapor barrier
13. galvanized sill flashing
14. fin tube radiator
15. plywood
16. prefabricated concrete panel
17. insulation in concrete joints
18. poured-in-place concrete

3
1. hardwood rail
2. steel T 80x40x5mm
3. wooden edge
4. wooden floor (teak)
5. rubber sheet
6. lead
7. rubber sheet
8. three layers roofing membrane
9. water drainage channel
10. synthetic foam insulation board (with integrated slope)
11. prefabricated concrete edge panel
12. high density insulation 60 mm
13. downspout with continuous chain
    between floor slabs
14. upper rail of moveable sunscreen
    (with electric controls at east elevation)
15. poured-in-place concrete slab

4
1. exterior wooden sliding door
2. synthetic raised flooring
3. wooden grating with metal angle frame
4. silicone sealant joint
5. prefabricated concrete floor tile
6. 30mm diameter holes at 100mm O.C.
7. rubber sheet
8. lower guide for sunscreens
9. anchor
10. downspout with continuous chain between floor slabs
11. vapor barrier
12. fin tube radiator
13. plenum
14. floor slab
15. insulation 60 mm
16. expansion joint
17. backer rod, silicone sealant joint
18. exterior wooden sliding panel

5
1. insulation sliding door
2. aluminum sheet metal
3. 46x67 framing
4. exterior wooden sliding door
5. wooden grating with metal angle frame
6. lead
7. fin tube radiator
8. plenum
9. poured-in-place concrete edge
10. synthetic foam insulation board
11. poured-in-place concrete
12. stainless steel anchor
13. fiberglass 85 mm double glass membrane
14. 100 mm sandy limestone
15. polyethylene sheet vapor barrier
16. insulation with intermittent compression blocks
17. 100 mm thick sandy limestone attached with 20 x 210 mm
    spring anchors at 400 mm O.C.
18. aluminium sheet metal

6
1. 100 mm thick sandy limestone panel
2. waterproof membrane
3. vapor barrier
4. rigid insulation
5. thickened slab edge supported on footing
6. footing

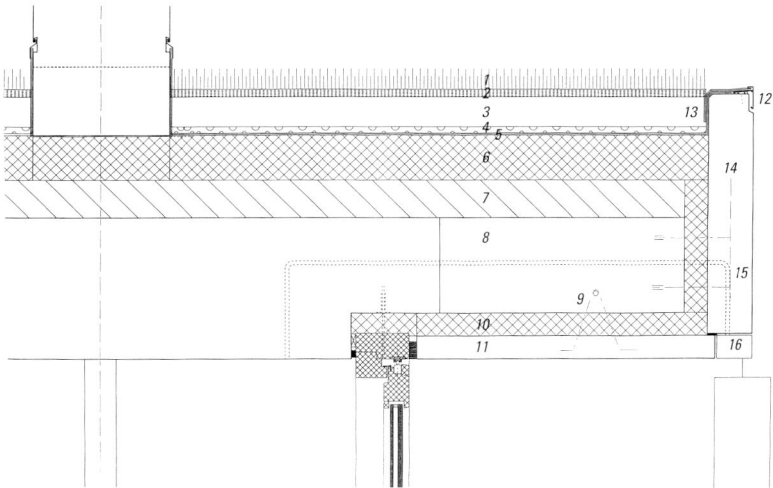

1

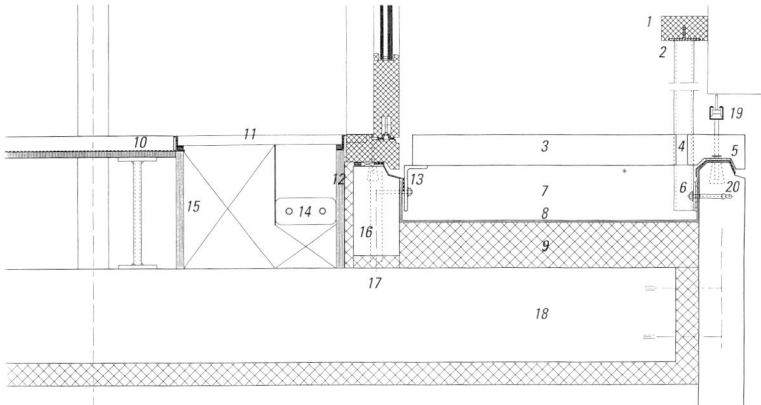

2

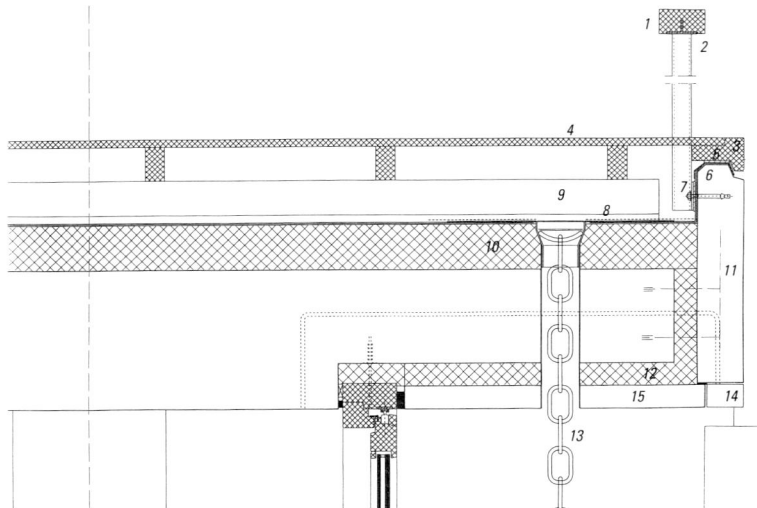

3

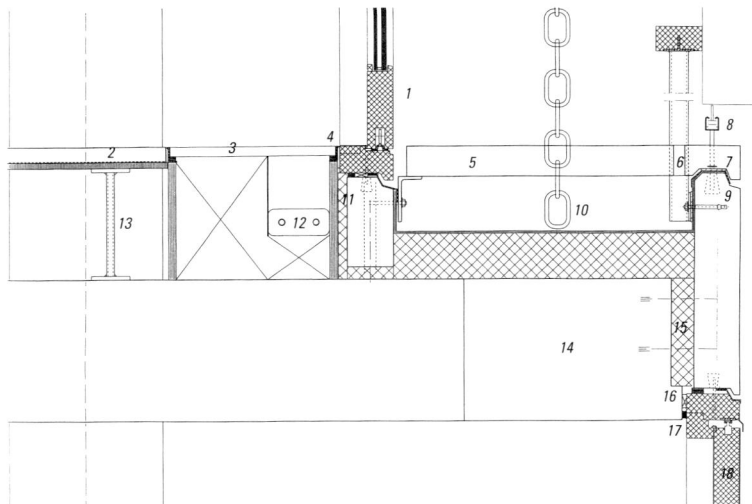

4

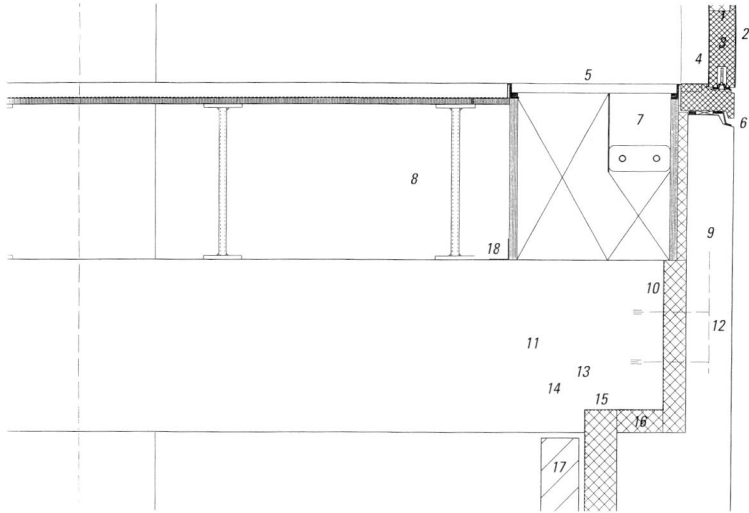

5

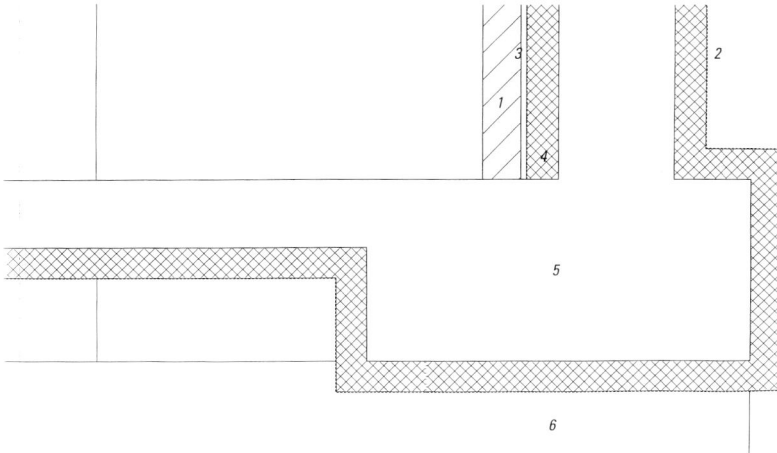

6

The spacious quality of the interior is reflected in a rose window of different types of glass.

net 3 ⟨

VPRO

RVU

NPS

VARA

VPRO

VARA / NPS

NET3

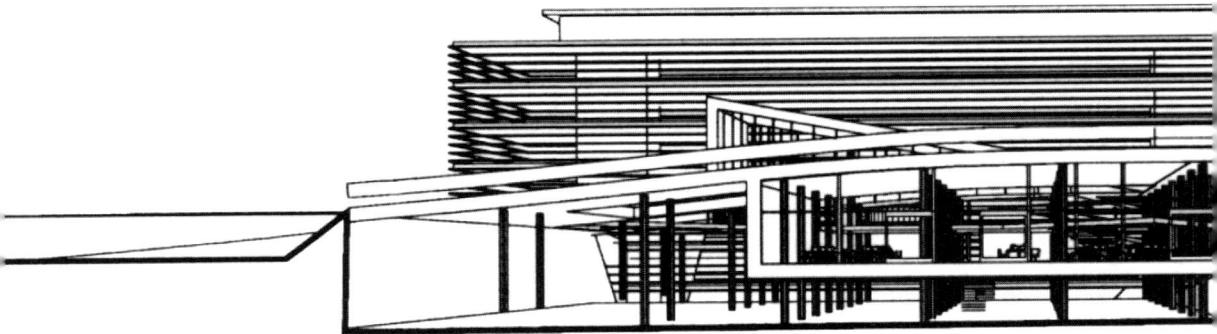

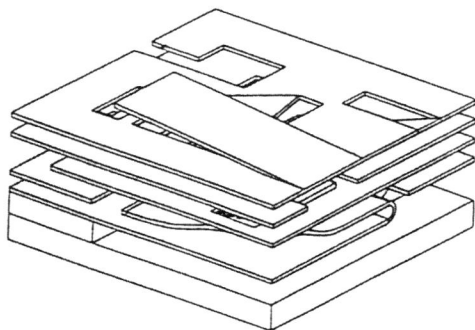

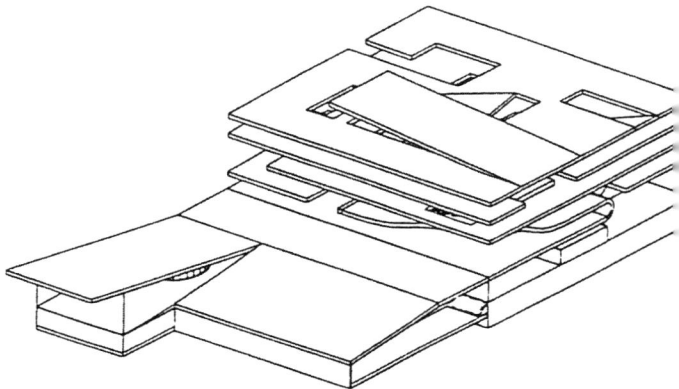

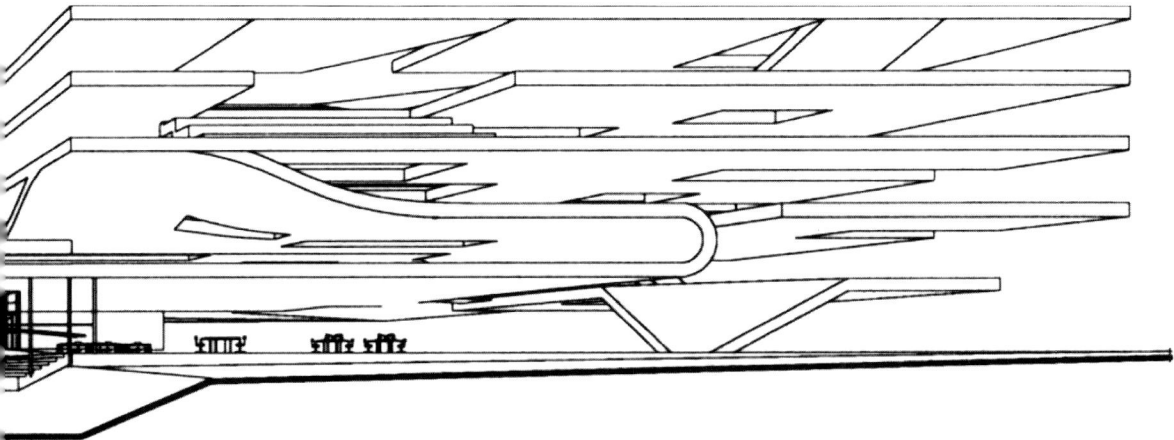

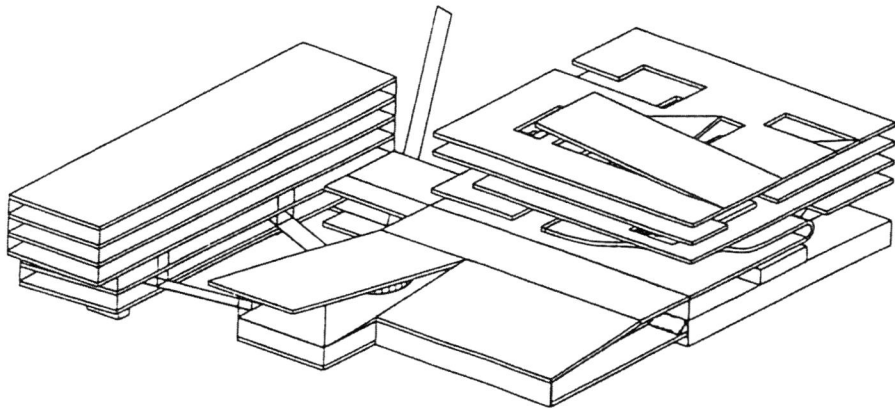

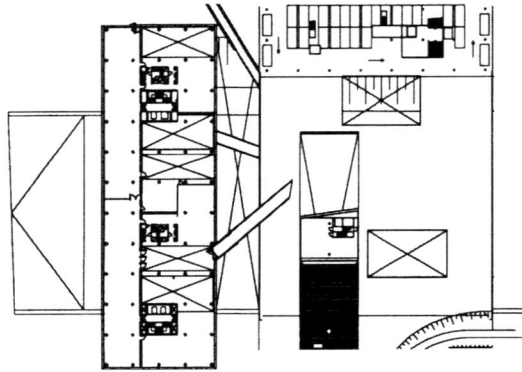

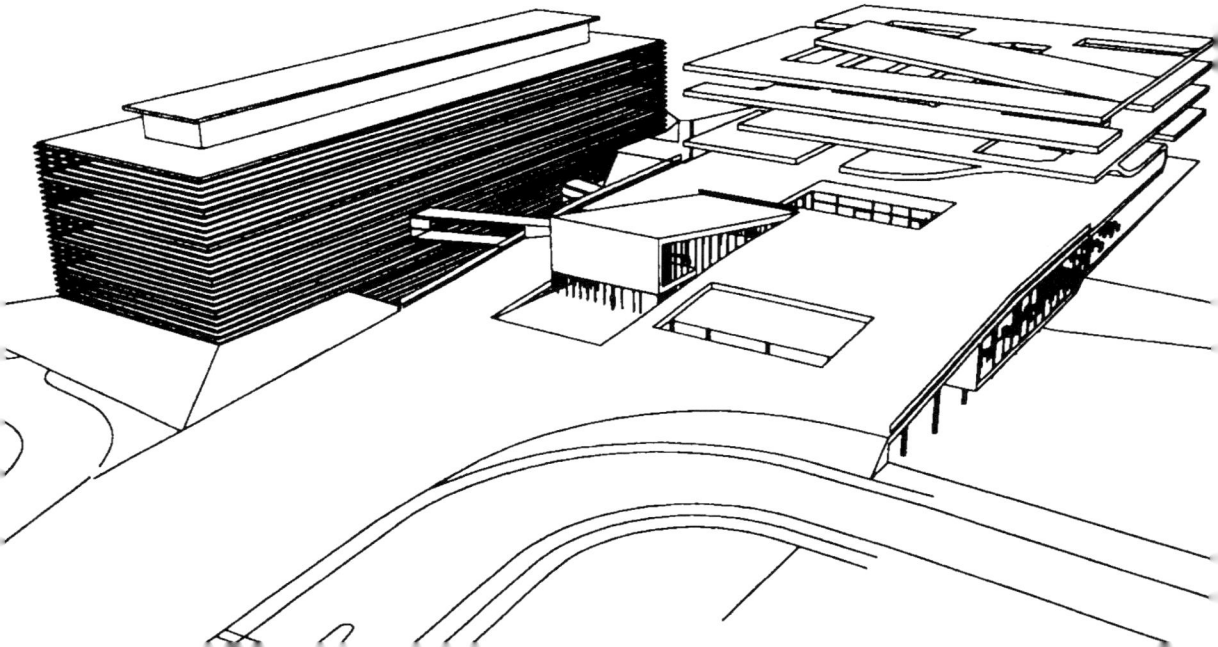

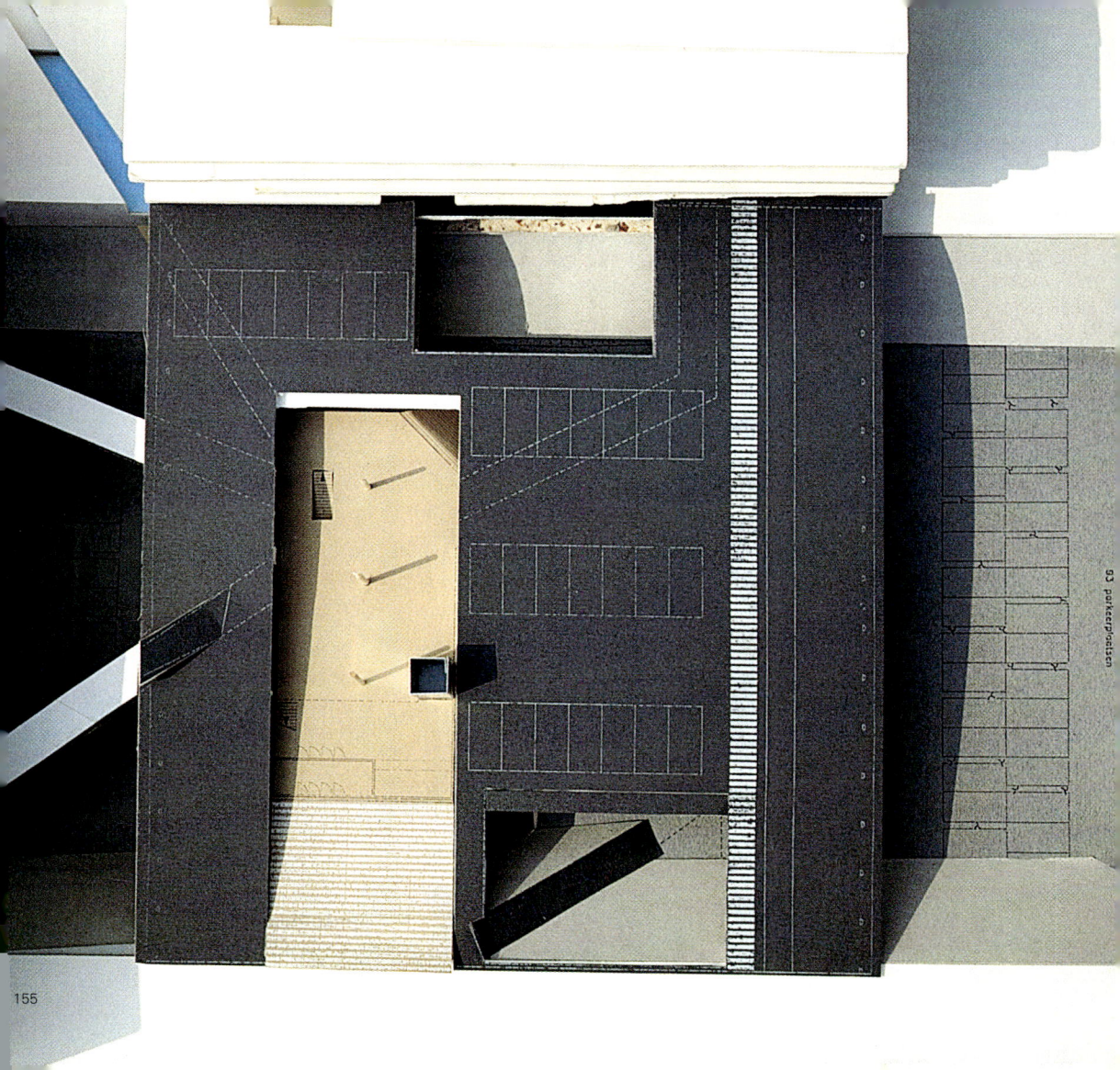

155

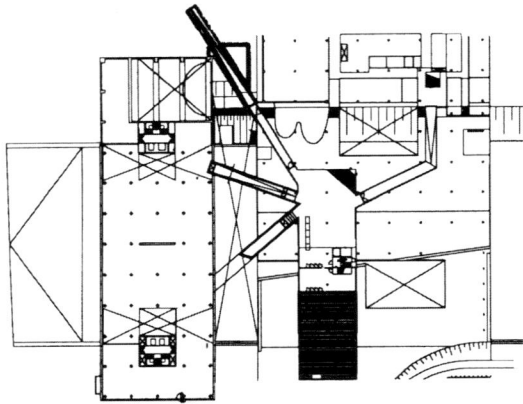

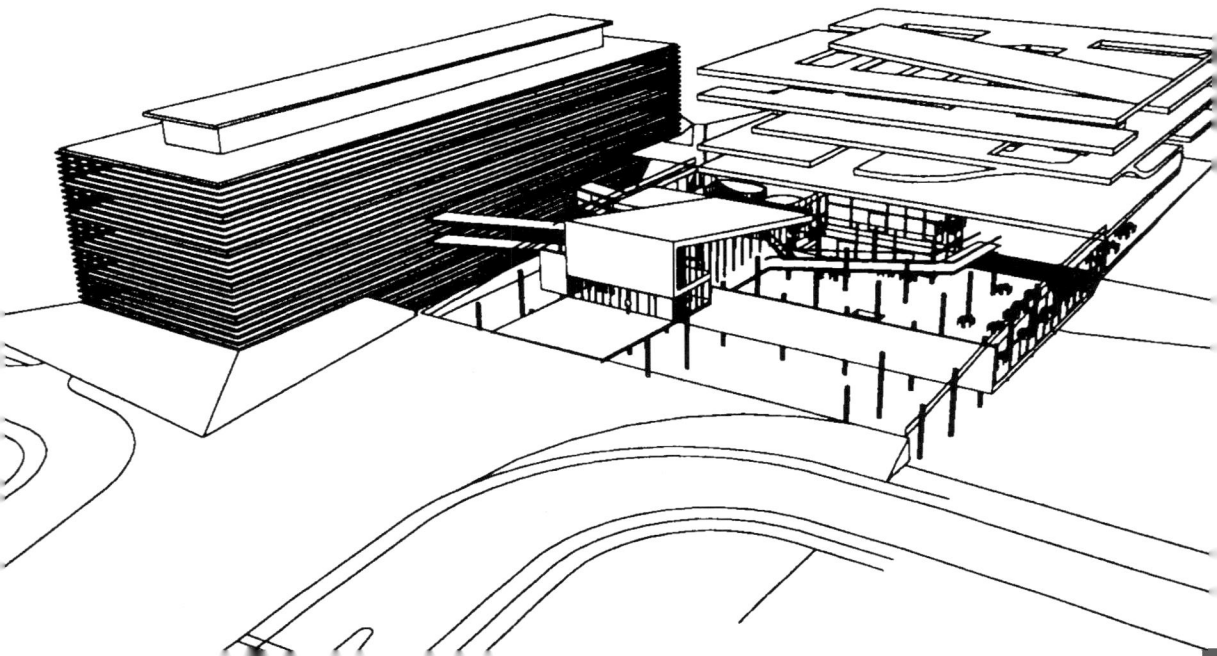

93 parkeerplaatsen

Workshops, offices

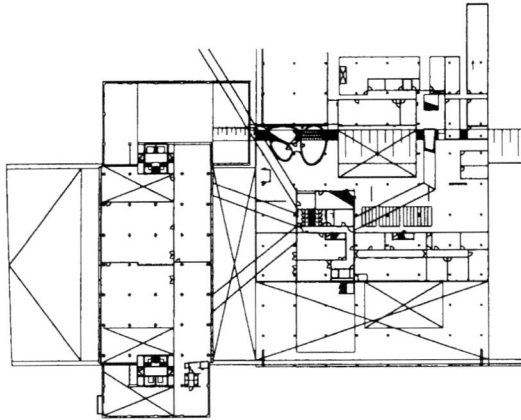

Valley. Car park

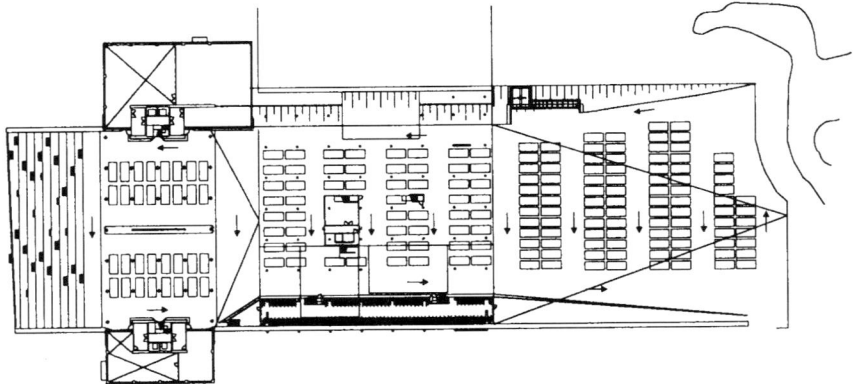

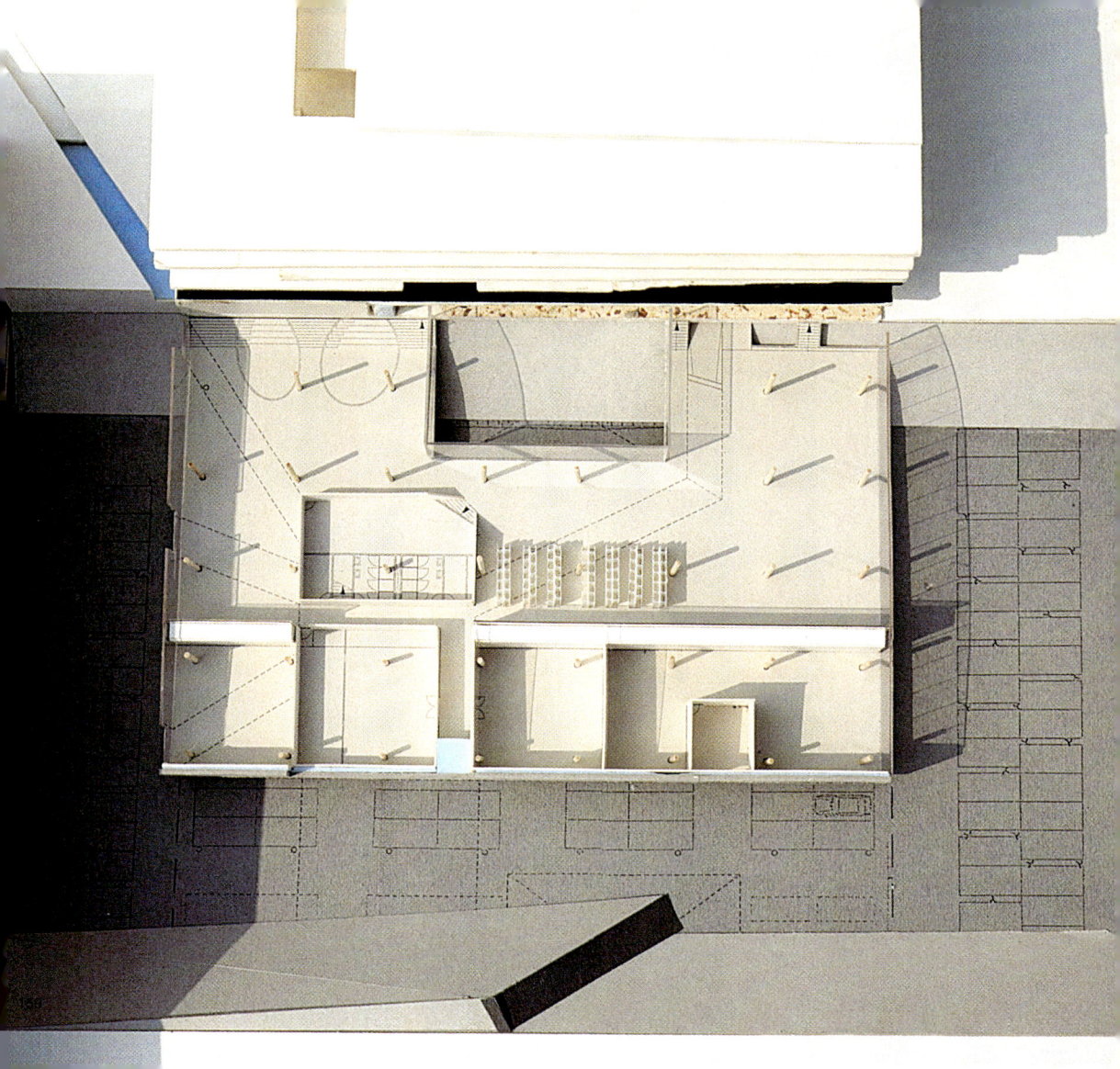

Today, one and a half year after the completion of the Villa, we start to see in how far the informality in organisation and the increase in scale can meet in the use of the villa as a metaphor. When one enters certain wings it still feels as if one enters one of the old villa's. Other parts now show almost the entire organisation, which is a completely new sensation, and was one of the goals of the client. The softening of some of the side effects of this massification have immediately demanded additions in the form of sound absorbing materials and some, mostly transparent, separations.

So while some of the inhabitant who still feel nostalgia for the silent old days are boxing off their private domains, others like the growing digital group, have embraced the buzz of the new Villa. And they meet in the restaurant, overlooking the Dutch broadcasting scene emerging in the surrounding Media Park.

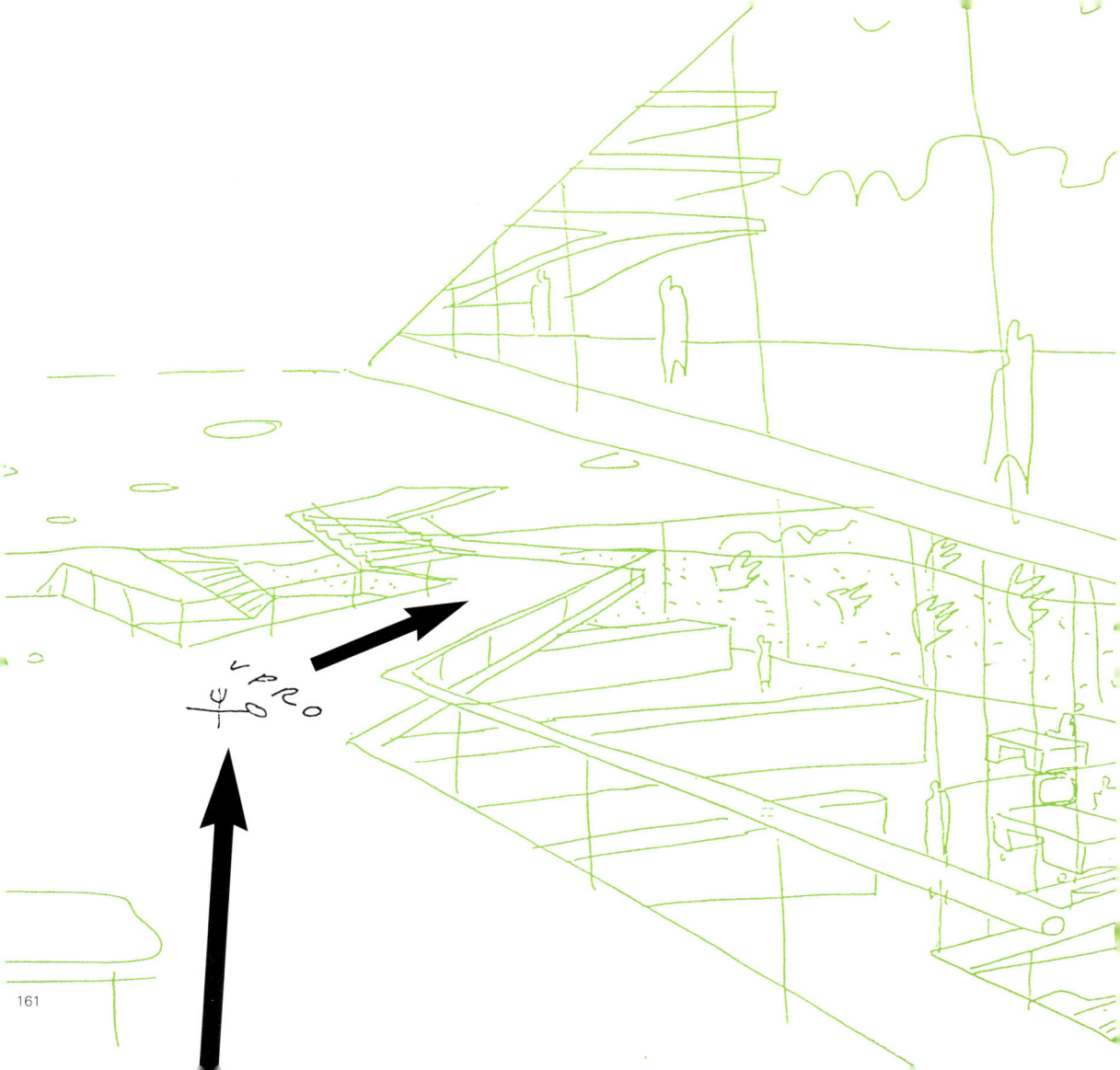

VPRO

sit coms

Preventive custody

Rafael Reig

The foxes have holes and the birds
of the air have nests, but the Son of man
hath not where to lay his head.
Matthew, 8: 20.

Your Honour, he had stuck the Phillips screwdriver into her heart.
The red plastic handle was still throbbing, like a pendulum, tick–tock,
tick–tock, tick–tock.
I was hypnotized, it seems to me, by the sight of Miss Hiddink's dead body.
Tick–tock, the screwdriver throbbed and I couldn't take my eyes off the
deceased woman's stockings. She was wearing garters: say no more.
Kluivert must have been in the garage, because I heard the unmistakable
bang–bang–bang of his Volkswagen. Jan was an ideas–man all the way.
Miss Hiddink, on the other hand, drove a Volvo and wore Dior trouser suits.
One of the scriptwriters would be up any minute from the basement, where
they were still filling their blackboards up with optional destinations,
unlike mine. What could I do? What was the answer?
I'm from Casas Ibáñez, your Honour, in Albacete, I'm completely herbivorous
and a keen reader of philosophy. I'm constantly perfecting my mind by
devouring printed matter, anything, even the instructions on medicine bottles.
I've read the whole of Ludwig Wittgenstein: say no more. Benito Navalón
Molina, at your service, though my friends called me Tinín, when I had friends
and a stone–built, whitewashed house with a garden and a coal fire for

cooking, and a mother, and help yourself to more. Since I left, I've devoted my entire life – every minute, your Honour – to finding somewhere to go back to, a home, a hand on which to rest my brow. I, too, would have liked to hear some day, "Darling, you work too hard!" or "You shouldn't let them take advantage of you, Benito, my sweet!". I'm not asking that much, but, please, don't get me wrong: it's what people call the Matthew effect, which regulates international finance and my own existence: "For unto every one that hath shall be given, and he shall have abundance: but from him that hath not shall be taken away even that which he hath" (Matthew, 25:29).

I know, my duty was to call the police. Or at least to get away. But don't get me wrong: I couldn't run away from home. Because the VPRO had finally become my home, your Honour.

So I stayed hypnotized, my eyes rivetted on the throbbing screwdriver, tick–tock, tick–tock, tick–tock, like a metronome between Miss Hiddink's breasts.

When I was twenty I left my parents' home on a bike, I left it on the bank, swam across the river and walked as far as Albacete, where I caught the bus for Germany. I found a job at Siemens, but they sacked me after a year: the bosses get uptight about workers who read Martin Heidegger in the canteen instead of eating those sausages which I don't even touch; as you know, I'm a metaphysical vegetarian from La Mancha.

I went halfway round Europe, walking miles, kilometres and versts, and begged for florins, francs, pounds sterling, marks and even roubles.

I was a *clochard* in Paris, a squatter in London, a *Landstreicher* from Berlin to Bonn... anything rather than go back to Casas Ibáñez without that Mercedes Benz, because then I would really have been a dead duck, the laughing stock of the town and of the whole province.

I used to hide in the metro to sleep, or in shops or municipal parks; I stuffed my shirt with the pages of *Sein und Zeit*, full of notes in the margins. They always found me after a couple of nights. Then it was back to square one. In Bonn, a story by Poe gave me an idea. If I made myself as visible as possible I'd end up being transparent. Rather like people who gatecrash weddings, and who don't need to hide because the groom's family think they're the bride's guests and vice versa.

Following this plan of operations I entered the Ministry of Finance, which I didn't leave for three years, until a caretaker reported me. That's life when you're a trespasser: once you leave home, you can't go back: say no more. So... it was back on the road again, beds made from cardboard boxes and fires in rubbish bins, until I managed to get into the Municipal Museum in Bruges, where I stayed for five years. A Japanese got me thrown out. I went back to the verges of the *Autobahn*, Heidegger under my clothes and wine in cartons. I got to Hilversum, and slept a few nights on the Mediapark building site, until I moved into VPRO after the bomb scare. They evacuated the building and I joined the people going back to work after the false alarm. As I'd expected, there was no surveillance. It was me who called, your Honour, putting on a typical skyjacker's voice. That's an offence, for example, isn't it?

At first, my new home unsettled me. I couldn't understand what it was they actually did there. Experience had taught me a golden rule: the form of a building follows, its function. So I couldn't help wondering what sordid or sublime activities called for a sloping floor or those stairs without handrails. And why wheren't there any corridors? Why did the windows always look onto other windows? Why did the building levitate, a few feet off the ground, but without touching? There was a glass wall. Translucent, then, to avoid any funny ideas: say no more.

The Ministry was an easily understandable building, perfectly adapted to its chief activity: sending bits of paper round a closed circuit of corridors, waiting rooms and offices. The museum had also been built with an obvious aim in mind: to give each visitor the chance to show he knew how to look at paintings all right, following the classical method of the right distance: if other people get close, you have to stand back and look at the painting from a distance; when they get further away, that's when you have to look at the canvas eyeball to eyeball, as though you were examining a single brushstroke. Open space is therefore an indispensable architectural element in a museum. Form and function as inseparable as ever.

At VPRO, I very soon realised, the only things that looked like what they really were were the computers and me. The rest was simulation. The offices tried hard not to look like offices, none of the desks had four legs the same and the bathrooms looked like lifts: say no more.

There were two groups of people there: the executives and the ideas–men.

The executives wore cufflinks, so as not to be tempted to roll up their shirtsleeves. The women wore high-heeled shoes. On the phone, they'd say "Speaking" when someone asked to speak to them, and sometimes they pretended to be speaking from a mobile phone:
"Hello, hello...! Are you receiving me?" they shouted. "Hello-hello... No coverage."
There never seemed to be coverage, but they insisted on going through the same farce several times a day.
What the ideas-men found most difficult was holding in their creativeness. However hard they tried, they couldn't keep it from showing through in some indescribable haircut. They wore sandals all the year round. Sandals and socks: say no more. In the basement, they wrote drafts for the scripts of television series. Three arrows came out of each character's name, with those optional destinies. For example, for Miss Overmars, in *The House of Love* (see page 292), they couldn't decide between: "(A) her own son fertilizes her in vitro by mail; (B) she goes to Cameroon with NGO cover as Maoist narco-guerrilla; (C) wakes up one morning to discover scar on abdomen: an organ is missing, stolen for clandestine transplant".
It was obvious, the building had been built with the purpose of combining two simultaneous simulations, as though the architects MVRDV were searching for the truth by piling fiction on top of fiction. When I realised that, I began to feel at home.
I lived in the open, so as not to rouse suspicion and to go unnoticed.

My face was familiar to everyone, but no-one could really say they knew me.
I established certain routines so as to control my ideal degree of visibility:
I wandered from room to room with a large folder, I put in an appearance in
the cafeteria and made a point of passing different people every time I went
to the bathroom. That's how I discovered something I would rather not have
known: Mr Kluivert's dressing habits. Or that he was having an affair with
Sabine Hiddink, the wife of Mr Bergkamp, the managing director.
I was happy trespassing at VPRO, until the day the architecture failed and
the inevitable collision took place: an ideas-man who destroys an executive,
as simple as that.
Typical Kluivert, was the first thing I thought. You'd expect him to kill by
hand, using weapons bought in an ironmonger's, a guy who tucks his shirt
inside his underpants.
To tell the truth, the fact that Jan Kluivert, from the news department, should
have murdered Sabine Hiddink, from administration, meant nothing to me
either way, seeing as I'm from La Mancha and a philosopher. That was their
business, but why did they have to commit their crimes right there in my home?
I stayed like that, hypnotized, looking at the body lying supine on its back.
I think I lifted the skirt. It was a reflex action, but it's also an offence, isn't it?
Tick-tock, tick-tock, tick-tock... clonk! The screwdriver vibrated like a
diapason, with the sound of the note A, stopped, and then I came to with a
start. "Ding-dong", I said to myself. "She's dead." Kluivert had done her in.
My situation was so desperate I decided to collaborate with the authorities.

If they didn't catch Kluivert, they'd go on looking and eventually discover me. But I couldn't report him either.

I thought a wrapping paper from the murderer's favourite chocolate bar would be enough help.

I didn't know Inspector Ooijier yet.

"Well, well! A *Kit-Kat*!" he exclaimed.

He picked up the wrapper, ate the remaining piece of chocolate, screwed up the silver paper in his hand and threw it into the waste-paper basket.

He had destroyed the evidence, just like that!

His assistant Reiziger asked for a list of the staff. His plan was to interview all the employees at VPRO one by one, check their alibis, investigate loose ends, carry out skillful interrogations, the way they do.

It was looking bleak for me. Don't get me wrong: I had to do something.

I remembered that Ooijier hadn't made a search of Hiddink's desk and that very night I crossed the police line. I was going to leave threatening notes signed by Kluivert in her diary.

A policeman caught me.

Once again I had to leave home.

I was innocent, everyone knows now. It was Jan Kluivert who tattooed a star on Sabine's heart, but I was sentenced to twenty years and one day: say no more.

By the time Kluivert confessed, last week, it was too late. Three months had gone by since I had discovered the essence of prison architecture.

This geometry of cells in straight lines, these rectangular yards, these window-less walls... form and function, essence and existence reconciled: the prison has been built with the one aim of allowing, by means of the straight line, pure thought, true freedom of spirit. It's the home of the *Dasein*: say no more. Last week, after supper (they only give me vegetables), at roll-call, I had an instantaneous *Seinsverständnis*: the understanding of the being! This is my home. Don't get me wrong: first a caretaker, then a Japanese tourist, then a murder... and now a free acquittal! To me, the order of release is like being banished, your Honour. This is my home: the exact form of true freedom. Bear in mind that, when all's said and done, I have committed offences. False phone calls for example. Contemplation of dead bodies for improper purposes. Isn't that enough? What about preventive custody, your Honour? I beg you. I could get up to terrible mischief, your Honour, I swear. I know exactly where I can get hold of some enriched uranium: say no more.

Signed: Benito Navalón Molina

May virtue return as deadly vengeance?

F. M.

I

The way Six would define himself is as follows: I am the man who is where he has to be, who does what he has to do, when he has to do it, because he has to do it. So neither the careful curvature of his fingernails, nor the elegant inflexions of his voice, which he uses no more than necessary, really fit in with the madness of the VPRO building.

Six would undoubtedly love to keep his exquisite order safe behind a door inscribed with his name; he undoubtedly hates having cars drive up a ramp into the heart of the building and park ten feet above what is supposedly his office. So it could be a quirk of fate that someone like Six should be working at Villa VPRO, that he should have got used to the see-through space in which other people's movements mess up his delicately arranged papers. And it's paradoxical that he should be the serials producer and look down his nose at the news department or the team that organises the competitions, as though his scorn could eliminate the element of chance they depend on, the entropy that unsettles and confuses him.

Because Six produces serials like an extension of his own certainty. Of course, he finds the overblown characters in the series absurd, the same as the unlikely twists of the script, such as the inclusion of three architects – apparently friends of the protagonists – who appeared one day out of the blue. He doesn't enjoy the high-sounding language the characters use, either, things you'd never hear him say, but it's his job and he helps put together each episode with the precision of an engineer. He hires the sets, squeezing the most out of every bargain and offer; he supervises the objects called for in the script as though they were part of his shopping-list.

Only once, in episode three hundred and twenty-four of the series, Six remembers with clenched teeth, one of the crucial elements of the scene was missing. Someone had stolen the dinner set on which the protagonists were to serve their umpteenth reconciliation meal: twenty-five pieces, including some wonderful glasses and the corresponding silver cutlery, of which one of the knives was to serve to bring about the tragedy.

Episode three hundred and twenty-four, which Six had gone over in his mind to the point of boredom, has the following plot: the three architects, friends of the protagonists, have been working hard to complete their new project: the *House of Love*. As on other occasions, they've used a huge amount of data, because it's through this cold agglomeration of reason that they manage to get their plan through to the other side, the side of the unexpected. In this case a construction which, on the basis of all the information they can get hold of about two lovers, the tastes and preferences they have in common, their happiest memories and an exhaustive examination of their letters, will serve to bring together a broken relationship. What better occasion that this to see if the house fulfils its mission, in episode three hundred and twenty-four of the series, in which the two protagonists agree to forget their differences over dinner.

The three architects prepare the scene thoroughly. They invite the lovers to the house of love, and there, surrounded by forms drawn by the imagination from the misty interior of desire, the two of them try for a reconciliation by candlelight. However, the wine upsets the architects' and the lovers' plans (and Six's, who hates these about-turns in the series). The atmosphere is spoilt when the hero, his voice clouded by the start of the third bottle, reminds her how, exactly forty-two episodes ago, she sold herself to the desires of a foul character, sneering and self- satisfied, someone with everything going for him, who shortly afterwards was found poisoned and nobody yet knows who did it. The heroine, for her part, her eyes ablaze with rage, mentions the time, three episodes later, when he was lying in a hospital bed faking illness (in that episode, the hero ended up getting off with the nurse in a famous scene which all the followers of the series remember). And so, after drowning their intentions in drink and opening up old wounds, episode three hundred and twenty-four ends in tragedy. From memories they come to blows, plates fly, the insults dig at the roots of ancient quarrels. The three architects, hiding wretchedly in the next room, have no choice but to listen as the crockery, the plan and the candles all come crashing down around them.

The dinner in episode three hundred and twenty-four took place without the dinner set it should have had. This is something only Six and his team know. The plates that got broken and the glasses that flew were bought in a rush, and the knife with which the hero fatally wounded the heroine wasn't silver, but ordinary stainless steel.

Six will never forget that episode, the theft, the affront. Especially when he's in his little laboratory at home, in which, with what could be termed amazing care and devotion, he has classified hundreds of poisons, in their corresponding flasks, with coloured labels that announce their properties: like belladonna, which acts on the central nervous system; or arsenic, which produces gastro-intestinal damage accompanied by pain and vomiting.

II

Alliances with fate tend to cause unexpected setbacks. Double-U knows this, but he's always had everything going for him, a valuable advantage sewn into the lining of destiny which has followed him from childhood. This may be why he has a smile on his face from morning till night. He likes his work, his family and his home, even though they're borrowed, even though he's buried the real ones under false images.

Double-U doesn't feel he's just an employee at VPRO: television is his life, the people at VPRO his family (except perhaps for Six), the building his home. He's been on the news team for years, and has come to mix reality with his reports in such a way that he thinks nothing happens other than what he broadcasts. The rest? The rest is an abstraction, the fun and games of distracted gods, which doesn't affect him or matter to him. So much so, that the only part of his existence he values out of all the minutes he's lived is what VPRO has broadcast, the rest doesn't count, it doesn't make any difference what happens off the screen.

Double-U and Six are different in every way. Six starts the day alone, entrenched behind his desk, without taking his eyes off his contracts and his diary. Double-U arrives halfway through the morning. He goes from one department to another with a broad smile and a friendly word for every computer and every glass of water. He doesn't need Six's tenacity, he never misses a news story, it's as though he could sense urgency in the ringing of a telephone, as though a generous conspiracy of fate dropped the scoop of the week on to his desk every time.

The chilly exchange of greetings between Six and Double-U has frozen with the passage of time. Especially after C-Aitch, Double-U's son, joined VPRO and became another success in his father's career. Life sometimes insists on drawing symmetries that later become asymmetrical, because Six's son, Nine, also tried for a job at VPRO, but Double-U intervened, because Nine, as Double-U made a point of demonstrating, is an idler, a troublemaker who every night crosses the line on the glass where alcohol sets the border with danger.

It's true, Nine is a dissolute young drunk, who comes in legless in the early morning thinking about his enemies and goes into his father's laboratory. He likes sniffing around in there, fingering the labels on the flasks of poison.

III

Although he hasn't been long at VPRO, C–Aitch and his team have got the biggest audience of any competition programme. The figures keep climbing and the advertising companies will do anything to snatch a few minutes out of the breaks in the programme. C–Aitch's idea is as follows: since we bring television into the home, why not bring the home into television?
The competition is broadcast once a week. Coordinated from the VPRO building, last week's winners are invited to the Media Park studios. And it is they who are most surprised when the VPRO mobile unit starts to move, following a random course established with the help of the games invented by C–Aitch: point blindfolded to a district on a map; indicate a left or right turn of the vehicle by counting the number of letters in a word.
After numerous aimless digressions, the car stops and the competition reaches its climax. Half the hearts in the city miss a beat as the journalist steps out of the car. Microphone in hand, accompanied by a cameraman and following instructions from Media Park, he rings a doorbell, goes in to the hall, up the stairs, presses a bell singled out by chance, shows the door opening and a noisy family appears, with the television switched on and tuned to the VPRO channel, which has chosen them, which is broadcasting their excitement and their furniture live.
Yes, there are also times when chance foils the triumphal scene and a woman in a dressing–gown, backed by a dour–looking husband, says she doesn't

understand, she doesn't know anything about any competition, she doesn't want them doing adverts in her house. But this adds to the programme's interest, because the spectators know that next week the prize will be doubled and that luck could bring VPRO into their home. And vice versa.

IV

What can she do with her family, with her home, wonders Double-L, Double-U's wife, as she reads a nursing magazine detailing the preparation of several poisons. She's been suspecting infidelities for some time, but none as persistent as this one. Before, they were just sporadic betrayals, given away every now and then by a trace of lipstick or a hair on his clothes. Now, the clues arrive as regular as a calendar, cruel and irrefutable. On Thursdays a new scent comes into Double-L's bedroom: a woman's perfume clinging to the revolting shirts her husband wears. Double-L used to be a nurse, and what is she now, she wonders as she reads distractedly that fifty percent of human poisonings are produced by household products such as aspirins, barbiturates, insecticides and cosmetics. Now she's nothing. She raises her head and looks at the untidy living-room, full ashtrays, remains of food left around by both father and son. Now she's nothing, she thinks as she hates her home, her husband and the god-damned television which, to cap it all, has stolen her son from her and leaves her alone every day, watching as the rooms shrink, the photographs on the television set laugh at her, the electrical appliances ogle her.

It's some time since Double-L gave up her job at the hospital, forced to stay home by the needs of her son and her home. Double-U didn't have time: that's television, he'd say to her. And so, almost happily, she took charge of the house and C-Aitch. She would go shopping, clean the house, pamper C-Aitch and prepare his snacks. But time has taken C-Aitch to his father's side, he no longer has time for her: that's telelvision, he says to her.

The loneliness, the infidelities and the constant arguments with Double-U have left Double-L with a bottle in her hands, the final result of an equation which, following the separation from her son, has gone from disagreeable to sordid. And it happens that barbiturates are easy to get hold of and that their effects can be fatal when mixed with alcohol or other drugs...

The magazine falls to the floor, next to a fossilized sandwich. The effect of the sixth gin is clouding her vision. She lies back on the sofa as she thinks about the man who spoke to her of the potent effects of pharmaceutical products: Six, a colleague of Double-U's, whom she met at the VPRO anniversary. Double-L remembers that it seemed strange to her to collect poisons, but Six talked about them with such feeling that his words became more and more exciting with each sip of gin. Double- L was impressed by Six from the first moment: the perfect cut of the suit, the tie – neither too loud nor over-serious –, the manicured nails, elegant manners. Lying back on the sofa, Double-L tells herself that if Six were her husband everything would be different: no more dirt, no more loneliness, no more gin.

V

Threena Half, Six's wife, is ambitious beyond limits. She demands her whims like orders and verges on violence if questioned. She's not past poisoning anyone who comes between her and what she wants. In fact, divorce is more and more of an uphill task for her and recently she finds that getting rid of her lovers is an odious business. Because Threena has always considered herself more than half a couple, and when she's been some time with a man the urge to leave him overpowers her. That's why, recently, she opens the door of her husband's laboratory, picks up a flask and reads the label yawning. A VPRO addict, Threena started buying any product she saw in the advertisements, but she wanted more. She's always looked favourably on the people in the news department, but when the serial started, which Threena Half followed as if her life depended on it, she did everything she could to get close to the hero (who was later her lover for several weeks). In the process, she had to marry Six, but that means nothing to Threena, she's used to mixing her whims and life, and she really does well out of her desires, which seem to have no bounds. After all, Six has given her money, a son only she wanted (and who now, after the fantastic education she's given him, she rejects and scorns), as well as a splendid house.

When the architects in the series talked about the house of love, it's hardly surprising that Threena should have decided that that was the sort of place she ought to be living in. None of Six's numerous arguments managed to convince her. Threena brought up her misfortune at having a son like Nine, obviously his father's fault, and that was the end of the matter. So they hired three architects and they told them everything they could imagine, hope for and remember, while Six filled in mortgage applications.

The house, after thousands of discussions and arguments, was so original that it was even used as the setting for episode three hundred and twenty-four of the series, in the murder scene.

VI

"Give me what's mine, and let time decide how we are to die", says the hero, and with this, episode six hundred and forty-eight of the VPRO serial comes to an end.

The background hiss blends with a sigh from Six, who as usual has held his breath for the duration of the programme. He gets up, slapping his papers with a satisfied feeling and leaves them perfectly stacked on the desk.

The episode was perfect, everything was just right, and the spectre of the stolen dinner set is kept at bay another day, like a needlessly troublesome worry.

The monitors at the back of the hall have swallowed up the credits and now the advertisements come on. At Villa VPRO the tension changes place with the same precision with which the clocks show the fifteen hours a week of broadcasting time. A moment ago Six's team, on the ground floor, was a bundle of nerves. Now, as chance will have it, the programme times have established that the competition should go next, and the uneasiness has moved up two flights of stairs, has moved along the invisible computer network that controls the building's thinking and has broken out in C-Aitch's team's area, where several people are clutching timepieces behind the glass screens.

Their anguish relieved, the members of Six's team stand talking.

The conversation outlines the next episodes. Although they don't have to put up with the infernal uncertainties of live broadcasting, it really makes no difference, because each episode calls for a balance between the script and the budget, and they only just have time for the daily miracle of filming things more or less as they want them. A large part of those minor miracles, as the team knows, are a result of Six's discipline, of his ceaseless working, which keeps him taking notes now that the others are saying they'll see him tomorrow.

Although the sound on his monitor is turned down, Six keeps one eye on the screen as he picks up his briefcase and closes the drawer of his desk. In the competition programme, the VPRO mobile unit is coming to its unforeseeable destination. Six's eyes widen as he recognizes his neighbourhood.

A shiver runs down his spine when he sees his street, his front door, his entrance hall and the door of his flat. He jumps to turn the sound on the television up and hears his son, Nine, completely drunk, cackling as he lets the journalists in. Then Six sees his books and his pictures, and follows with his eyes his son's back as he leads the cameraman to the room in which, according to Nine,   the television is on, the vital proof needed to qualify for the prize.

A murmur runs through every floor of VPRO, from the basement up to the roof lawn that crowns the top of the building. A surge of whispered voices, of hands covering mouths while Six's silhouette can be seen hurrying past the metallic panels, the windows, along the ramp leading to the car park. His solemn expression can be seen from every desk, a familiar look, now accompanied by haste and something that looks dangerously like rage. When Six gets into the car, a television hanging over the coffee machine at the entrance still shows his house, his bedroom, his wife, wrapped in red silk and tied to the bed, next to Double-U. The pictures show the remains of supper; there seems to have been a violent argument, because part of the dinner set is broken: beautiful pieces, with the corresponding silver cutlery. Completing the scene, with a glass in his hand, is Nine. He demands the prize in a loud voice and laughs as he points at the television set in Six's room, which multiplies the situation to infinity, a picture within a picture within a picture within a picture.

VII

Keeping the car only just within the limits indicated by signs and lights, Six
gets to the house of love. Although it's some time since the broadcast was cut
short, the cameraman is still sending pictures to VPRO. When Six gets to the
bedroom his wife is still tied to the bed screaming; nobody seems to be taking
much notice of her.
"Give me what's mine and let time decide how we are to die", says Six looking
scornfully at Double-U, and he starts to take the dinner set. The last thing
he picks up is a knife. A muffled scream runs through the rooms at VPRO.
The spectre of episode three hundred and twenty-four crosses everyone's
mind as Six cuts his wife free. A little later he leaves the house, gets into
the car and drives off calmly, the dinner set tinkling on the back seat.
Just as Six is leaving, the camera shows Double-U doubled up with pain.
He clutches his stomach with his hands and falls to the ground on his knees.
Maybe it was something he ate.

The true story of Bertrand Romaild

Luis G. Martín

I

The story of the Belgian architect Bertrand Romaild, retold by so many chroniclers in recent years, has been built up out of a handful of reliable accounts. He only gave one interview, full of obscure points and mysteries. Also, many of the documents mentioned in the descriptions of events – the contract with the VPRO television station, the letter from the director of programmes – have never been publicly reproduced and their existence is therefore doubtful. The digital disks of the most eloquent recordings were, of course, destroyed. And there is also evidence that one of the books about the case published just after the events – *De Waarheid over Bertrand Romaild* – distorted various episodes with sinister fantasies.

Romaild, it seems, had never heard about those living television programmes until the very day of his wedding. That day, a guest whose identity we can not be sure of confessed, in the midst of drunken laughter, that he had paid for his wedding and the honeymoon – a long and very expensive trip to the East – with the money he got for the broadcasting rights for his wedding night. Romaild thought it was a joke or just drunken bragging, and to humour him he laughed. That night, though, at the hotel, as he lay over his wife's body and began kissing her, he suddenly imagined that one or more hidden cameras were filming them from different corners of the room.

Although it was summer and it was a warm night, he pulled up the bedclothes to cover their bodies, but in spite of this precaution he began shivering, and his naked skin, from his face down to the tip of his toes, was gradually covered with cold perspiration like a feverish sweat. He was unable to go through with the sexual act or to sleep, as the idea kept coming into his head that although they were protected by the dark and the sheets, someone was watching them on a screen. The next day they travelled to New York and Romaild forgot all about it.

Almost a year later, as he himself remembered it, he discovered on a visit that his elderly mother was a subscriber to various stations broadcasting living television programmes. It was in her house, on the giant screen of her television set, that he saw one for the first time: a young boy of about sixteen or seventeen was sitting at a desk studying. Behind him, on the other side of the room, was the bed, unmade, and next to it, beside a window from which the street could be seen, was a stereo set and some loose records. At the top of the television screen were ten smaller pictures reproducing the same scene from different angles. At the bottom there were six pictures, one for each of the remaining rooms in the house: the main bedroom, another bedroom almost unfurnished, the living room, the kitchen and the two bathrooms. Using the remote control, the spectator could choose which room he wanted to go into and then, once there, which camera he wanted to watch from. When the boy got up from the table and opened a cupboard full of clothes, Romaild's mother changed angle to follow him, and then, when he headed for the bathroom with the chosen clothes to have a shower, she selected the new room and the successive angles of vision from which she could see him best. Then they saw how someone else arrived at the house – a woman, the boy's mother, perhaps –, poured herself a glass of wine, sat on the living room sofa and phoned someone. Her voice, like the rest of the sounds in the house, could be heard perfectly: she was speaking to the other person about another woman's illness, cancer.

At that moment Bertrand Romaild felt slightly afraid, a touch of nausea, but he said nothing. He vaguely remembered that many years before, when he was still a boy, he used to watch the house opposite from his bedroom window through binoculars, and sometimes, after a patient vigil, its rooms would offer up some of its secrets: an erotic encounter, weeping, a private vice, an argument or a fight. But he also got a strange pleasure from just watching the vulgarities of daily life: a boy doing exercises every morning, children playing, the care and skill with which a woman cooked, a servant's housework, the old folks taking a nap, family get–togethers, meals. When he met these people in the street, or in a shop, it gave him a feeling of satisfaction and a gentle thrill. Then, as he grew up, other juvenile perversions made him forget those childhood days when he spent hours watching engrossed the shadows on the windows of the house.

His mother told him about the family on television and two more she could visit on her subscription. She told him how many members each family had, the friends or acquaintances they had dealings with, how they spent the time, what they worked at or what the children studied, their problems, their oddities or obsessions, their good points, their sins, their infidelities, their immodesties, their hurts. The position they slept in, the clothes they wore, their illnesses. Romaild confessed later – in that one interview that seems definitely genuine – that when he heard all that he felt an evil joy, a dirty, murky feeling he was immediately ashamed of. He gave his mother and affectionate scolding for wasting time with these unhealthy frivolities, but to Nathalie, his wife, he said nothing of what he was thinking. When he got home, he suddenly imagined, like on his wedding night, that someone was watching them from a distance, and that night, while he had supper, brushed his teeth and undressed for bed, he felt afraid. He put the book he was reading face down on the bedside table so that no-one could see the title. When he switched off the light, though, he discovered that this fear excited him. Taking care not to mess up the bedclothes, he turned to Nathalie, undressed her completely and sodomized her in silence without a word of explanation.

Contrary to what almost all the chroniclers say, there is no indication that in the subsequent months Bertrand Romaild saw any more living programmes on television, though it's probable that he did. In December, Nathalie and he travelled with his boss, the architect Atte Klerk, to Hilversum. They had to attend a reception the North-American company LieverNine was giving for the Dutch high society to celebrate their takeover during the last three years of more than half the media in the country including the television channel VPRO, in whose building the reception was held. It was at this party that he met Arjan Van Wijk, the man the LieverNine executives had chosen to direct the channel's new programmes. Van Wijk politely praised Nathalie's beauty and talked with Romaild for more than an hour. He answered his questions amicably and went into all the details of the living programmes, including some which were highly confidential as they were considered a professional secret. Van Wijk, who was usually distrustful and little given to sharing secrets with anyone, nevertheless seemed inspired and talkative that evening. He was charming with Nathalie and trusting with Romaild. He spoke at length and cheerfully and even livened up the conversation with stories and jokes, something which those who knew him well found quite extraordinary.

Van Wijk himself gave an account of that meeting later, so that we are in no doubt about what was said. The programmes director confessed to Romaild and his wife that it was he in person – with no go-betweens or delegates –

who hired the people who wanted to feature in the living programmes. Some of them were convinced that by showing off their dramatic talents the doors to more highly valued artistic work would be opened to them: the cinema, the theatre or the comedy series on television itself. Others, lonely beings or the poor in spirit, were only looking for affection, and they were satisfied with the knowledge that so many people knew of their troubles and sympathized with them. Most of the people who asked to have their lives televised, however, were in need of money. Unemployed people of uncertain age, no longer able to find work, approached the channel and offered their privacy as merchandise. It was well-paid, although the remunerations in each case depended on a series of circumstances. There were a lot of living programmes that were actually faked: the producers of the television channel built stage sets imitating the homes of different types of family and hired people to act out their lives. They were almost like dramatic series. These accidental actors played a part. They didn't follow the thread of any script, so much as patterns of behaviour that the scriptwriters outlined for them. They worked with other actors, whom they had to treat exactly as though they were members of the same family, with no holds barred. Husband and wife, for example, had full sexual relations, and the children obeyed their parents' every whim. They were also given a make-believe occupation and leisure habits: trips to the cinema, visits to friends, dinner parties, travel. When they were off the set of the house on these grounds, going to the office or keeping an appointment, they saw their real families. The channel was running more than fifty of these quasi-fictional series in which the actors depicted invented lives. Each one, obviously, was broadcast all day long without a break, and spectators who tuned in could see, as Romaild's mother had done, whichever room of the house they fancied at each moment. Audience figures were high, Van Wijk explained, because subscription rates were so cheap that even low-income groups could afford it. These programmes, though, were somehow lacking in interest, because none of what they showed had the same thrill as the real thing.

Genuine living programmes, as Van Wijk went on telling the Romailds, were the ones in which the television cameras were set up in the homes of real families who in return for payment agreed to be observed by others. Outwardly they looked the same, but spectators here knew that everything they saw on the screen – all the characters' feelings, arguments, tempers, envies, habits, passions and moods – was true, or, at least, no falser than what they themselves felt. When these broadcasts first began, the families were always shy and embarrassed, and didn't speak much or do anything that might compromise them. But later, as time went by and they got used to the glare of the cameras in the corners, they forgot about them and the people watching from their homes. Then they began to act naturally and show those weaknesses their audiences expected of them. Van Wijk's channel broadcast almost as many series of these as of the spurious type, because although the subscription rates were much higher, the thrill of discovering the joys and miseries of other lives attracted a lot of spectators. The more faithful subscribers were also able to take part, via a computer terminal, in decisions and events in the family home, urging the actors to accept or turn down a date, to invite a neighbour round more often or even to alter the decoration in the rooms. The channel made sure – with absolute rigour, Van Wijk stressed – that spectators' opinions were taken into account. Bertrand Romaild listened to the words of the programmes director with some fascination. Nathalie, for her part, being more apprehensive, already seemed to be on edge. But when Van Wijk paused at some length, suddenly stopped his bursts of drunken laughter and approached them with a glass of champagne half raised to his lips, the two understood that they had only heard the warm-up to what he had to tell them. The woman shuddered and grabbed her husband's arm. Van Wijk, his eyes glassy and unseeing, looked quietly at her. Then he went on talking.

Some people, he said, signed contracts with the channel to broadcast living programmes without the rest of the family's knowledge. The television cameras were set up under cover, with complicated camouflage, and highly sophisticated technology was used – infra-red lighting, long-wave directional microphones, digital sensors – to ensure that the recordings combined high performance with maximum discretion. They usually took advantage of a family holiday to work on the house undisturbed. When the occupiers got back, they found everything as they left it, but only superficially: everywhere, behind the walls, inside the computers and televisions sets, in the silver backing of the mirrors, in the filaments of the light bulbs or in the liquid crystal of the telephone screens, viewers, lenses and diaphragms were filming their movements and recording everything that happened. The pictures were startling. What the television showed was not only real but also had the freshness and triviality that always governs intimate actions. Nathalie blushed as she suddenly remembered, as though in a glow, the pet names she and Romaild called each other in private and the affectedness of their sentimental conversations, when they spoke with sham theatrical voices.

These films were never completely legal, of course, but participation in them by a member of the family exonerated the television channel from blame. Van Wijk, who had been chosen for the job by LieverNine because of his talent for getting round the law, admitted that they had on occasion been sentenced to pay the odd fine, but the profits to be made on this sort of living programme were beyond doubt. Although the cost of subscribing was very high, there was never any shortage of spectators. The television channel made money and the people who had negotiated this betrayal with them almost got rich. Leaning forward as if to rest his lips on the edge of the glass again, Van Wijk mentioned a figure that made the Romailds jump. It was only a rough figure, of course, because the final amount depended on the number of subscribers who paid to see the series, and that number depended in turn on the interest the exposure managed to rouse in the audience. Spectators who spent all that money on a television programme wouldn't make do with any old cheap rubbish. What they wanted were perversions, vice, powerful emotions. They demanded adultery or incest, law-breaking and immorality. Van Wijk, lowering his voice even more, told them of a few cases he remembered: a mother driven to satisfy her adolescent son sexually, a devout man who had to commit sacrilege every day, a judge forced to commit perjury, a middle-class woman who prostituted herself to sailors and villains, an ex-policeman who betrayed his colleagues. These aberrations were sometimes the idea of subscribers, who had the right to impose their preferences if the programme wasn't to their liking, but at other times it was the protagonists themselves who provoked them, greedy for more money. They knew that a series's fame spread quickly amongst followers of this sort of programme. Competition between them was ruthless: they had to be full of constant surprises to survive as audience favourites.

Arjan Van Wijk stopped suddenly and turned his head to look through the windows. The sky was completely overcast, but a white line of snow could be seen on the metal railings outside. In the surrounding fields, the grass would be frozen. The director of programmes sighed wearily, wet his lips with a finger dipped in champagne and then raised his hand ceremoniously towards Nathalie to ask her to dance. Followed by Bertrand, who was absent– mindedly turning all this over, they went down the curving slope on which a carpet had been laid out, crossed the crowded room and stepped on to the dance area as they turned to one another and began to dance. But Van Wijk's arms immediately went limp and he let go of the woman's waist and collapsed unconscious amongst the dancers.

Bertrand Romaild later said that that same night, as they drove back to Amsterdam, a vile idea had already crossed his mind. Like any respectable man, he lessened the horror by imagining that his culture, money and refinement would free him of any abominable temptation, and that those abject fantasies would therefore boil down to no more than intellectual amusement. Events, however, have shown that that wasn't the case.

One month later, at the end of January, Atte Klerk sacked Romaild from the firm of architects without a proper explanation. Romaild, perhaps from shame, said nothing to Nathalie. He visited other firms he knew and visited influential colleagues, but no–one would have him. For several weeks he carried on leaving home early as though he were going to work and then at supper speaking of new projects, clients and buildings. Although he was obviously at that moment turning over the idea of featuring in a living programme, he might never have dared to take the next step if his bank director hadn't started threatening him with seizure.

Romaild immediately asked for an appointment with Arjan Van Wijk, who at first couldn't remember him very well. He had to tell him it was his wife he was dancing with when he fainted at the LieverNine party. He travelled to Hilversum on Friday. Van Wijk was waiting for him in a large office closed in with glass panels and raised above the level of the large central hall. On hearing what it was he wanted to speak to him about, though, he got up from the chair and asked him to go with him. They talked as they made their way slowly amongst the tables in the building, coming and going as though they were taking a walk round a little garden. The place was teeming with people, filled with the sound of telephones and computer voices. Romaild looked at the windows, made from lots of different types of glass, and he noticed that at time of the morning, with the sun high in the sky, the light that shone through them – pale in places, sombre, amber or dazzling – was like handwriting. Without knowing why, he suddenly remembered the aging face of the architect Winy Maas, who he had seen years ago, when he was still an apprentice sketching lines on other people's drawings, and it seemed to him that the shape of his face, the line of his eyes and his lips, were like those of the building. Like the writing of unequal windows.

Van Wijk tried to persuade him not to go through with it, but finally, faced with his obstinacy, he agreed to help him. Although there were several deserving candidates that the channel would have to hire for the next few programmes, it was he, Van Wijk, who took the decisions and hired the candidates. He couldn't promise Romaild that he'd be chosen, but he could be sure he'd take their friendship and his unfortunate situation into account. He wanted to be sure of his determination, and he asked him what he imagined he would do when the cameras were connected. Van Wijk confessed later that although Romaild's answer was vague and not very bright, the depraved, lecherous look with which he drew the scene convinced him that his would be an excellent series.

Weeks before the start of his living programme, Romaild began behaving as though the television cameras were already broadcasting. He came home with a repulsive prostitute – huge thighs covered in varicose veins, breasts swollen with fat, blackened teeth – and committed all sorts of brutality with her in his wedding bed. He left clues so that Nathalie would realise, and when she plucked up courage to ask him, after some doubts and shame, he answered angrily and got furious. Sometimes he hit her.

This became normal treatment once the programme had started, after a week's holiday they took in a hurry so that the technicians could set up the cameras in the house (at the end of April; the airline tickets and check-in from the hotel they stayed in in Tunis have been kept). Romaild turned out to have an unusually libertine imagination, according to those who were able to see the digital recordings before they were destroyed. Having made Nathalie suspicious that he was unfaithful, he sent a man – one of those barroom braggarts who'll do anything for money – to seduce her. Out of disgust rather than morality, Nathalie resisted for some time, but Romaild gave the ape the necessary instructions each day so that he gradually won her over, and eventually, when she could no longer stand the misery, she gave in. In the following weeks, Romaild redoubled his cruelty so that Nathalie, distraught, threw herself into her lover's arms once and for all. Then, when he had succeeded, he went back to treating her with the sweetness he had always felt for her. At that point she broke down. She couldn't speak for days. She was trapped in a long dream, in a shadow. The programme got so many subscriptions that within three months it had a bigger audience than any other, although the prices, set by the company according to how spectacular each series was, were also some of the highest. Romaild started receiving massive cheques, and the money, as well as serving to multiply his atrocities and make them even more sophisticated, also provided him with a sort of spiritual relief that eased his remorse.

Arjan Van Wijk wrote to him, according to written accounts, congratulating him on his success and letting him know the spectators' requests so that he could take them into account. He recommended that he keep acting as he had until then and sent his best wishes.

Long before the end, Romaild realised that life was over for him. During his moments alone, resting, unconcealed from the spectators, he exhibited a lively, almost jubilant anguish. His hands shook like a drunkard's, he couldn't sleep more than an hour at a time and he hardly ate, but his emaciated face retained an air of felicity. He had a strange expression, like a cardsharper at the roulette table or a puritan before forn cating: a vacant grin in which pleasure and repentance seem to be one and the same thing. He remembered a time when he had loved Nathalie passionately. Now he didn't even feel sorry for her as she lay in a senseless heap on the bed or when he heard her delirious wailing. He watched her silently on the screen of a television set he had had installed in a closed room so that the spectators could see him suffering for the pain his works had caused. It was one of the film effects Van Wijk most praised: that view of smaller and smaller figures – the spectator, Romaild, Nathalie – watching on television the pain they have caused.

He killed her out of pity for himself. To be able to sleep again. But nobody knows exactly how he did it, because that day, after committing every sort of act of violence and depravity before the gaze of paying strangers, he disconnected the computerized filming system for thirty minutes. When transmission resumed, Nathalie was dead and bleeding on the bed, and he had disappeared.

II

It's been proved that Arjan Van Wijk had never heard of Bertrand Romaild before that December night when they met. They hadn't coincided at previous LieverNine celebrations, to which Romaild hadn't been invited, or at social events in Amsterdam. When they were introduced by chance at the Hilversum party, Van Wijk, who was already feeling a bit tipsy, tried to get rid of him by politely ignoring him, but when he saw Nathalie with him he was dumbstruck and smiled in amazement, with a daft look on his face. He started talking carelessly to them, so that they wouldn't go away, and not being a captivating, worldly man who knew how to keep people entertained with wit or amusing small talk, he ended up talking about his work. But he discovered, with surprise, that Romaild found this shady business extremely interesting, and he therefore went on telling him everything he wanted to know, even a few murky exaggerations he made up to impress him.

Van Wijk wasn't married. He had never loved anybody, so far as he could tell, although he had capriciously courted certain women who struck him as beautiful. But contemplating Nathalie that evening he had a feeling of dread, sadness and surprise. He pretended to speak to Romaild so that he could look at her. However, he could do no more than pay her polite compliments so as not to seem rude, and later, spurred on by the champagne, ask her to dance. When he took her in his arms he felt terrified. Then he fainted.

Love at a distance often engenders boredom, especially in someone who has never felt inner peace. Arjan Van Wijk gave in to envy and fear. Every day for a week he sent Nathalie roses anonymously, trusting that she would guess. He got no answer and he thought her silence was an affront. Then he started to plan his revenge for an offence no-one had committed. It wasn't easy to convince Atte Klerk to sack Romaild from the firm of architects and use his influence to make sure no-one else hired him. With the help of the station's sponsors, who didn't know what it was they were lending their favours to, he got the architect's bank to threaten him with seizure. Then he sat down to wait. He spent eleven days shut in his office in Hilversum, looking out through the big windows at the fresh green of the countryside. Finally, Romaild phoned him to ask for an appointment. The director of programmes had fixed everything so that his wishes could be fulfilled as soon as possible. At the interview with Romaild, which he held in the station's editorial office, strolling amongst the tables as though it were an everyday affair, he saw that he hadn't been wrong in his hunch: the architect, with his gently lascivious, debauched look, would do anything necessary to satisfy him. He gave instructions to the producers and started to imagine what would happen.

Van Wijk was the only person who saw the Romaild series. There were no more subscribers. The money to pay for it out of his private fortune, built up in the course of his profession and from a few discreet frauds. For the three months the broadcasts lasted, he was out of the way, shamming serious illnesses or long trips that kept him away from Hilversum. Shut away in his house in Amsterdam, he spent the day in front of one or other of the television screens he had in every room. When he slept, taking advantage of a moment when the Romailds were away, he left the volume turned up full so that the sound of their return would wake him.

Arjan Van Wijk was happy for the first time in his life watching Nathalie Romaild being ill-treated. The sight of her naked body and her long legs and delicate feet fascinated him. He watched dry-mouthed as the men – her husband or the ape he had hired – opened her thighs to cover her, or how they turned her over and held her arms, twisting them as they sodomized her. Van Wijk, who was almost an old man, was long past the age when people are ashamed of the pleasure they find in other people's suffering. He had no second thoughts and felt no remorse. He wrote to Romaild, on behalf of the series's audience, demanding that he commit all the monstrosities he had ever dreamt of. He knew at once that Nathalie was going to die, but he didn't notice when it happened. He kept looking at the screen, trying once again to fathom the mysteries of beauty when it could even persist in a dirty, emaciated face running with blood.

Late night

Lola Beccaria

Anita couldn't stop squeezing the coffee cup and anxiously sliding her fingers over the porcelain, up and down and down and up. It was a long time since she'd touched a man's body. She had taken up celibacy as an emergency measure, a drastic solution to her usual sentimental disasters, joining the club for people who don't screw so as to keep from getting hung up, so as not to suffer. She had two degrees, a high I.Q., a nice face and a good figure, but her particular male canon always had a lethal effect on the continuity of her relationships: she invariable felt attracted to undomesticated men, the type with broad, sweaty shoulders, a back like a wardrobe cupboard, long legs and firm buttocks. Her amatory curriculum at that stage of the game, for example, included a Portuguese lorry driver, a Polish bricklayer and an Athenian dockhand. Drawing on the hypothesis that between men and women there is no room for understanding, she almost preferred them to speak an unknown language, so as to emphasize the communication of instincts and skirt the multiple pitfalls of spoken language. That very morning Maurice had dropped in at the offices of the magazine that paid his keep. He had just been commissioned to take some photographs to illustrate an article. His love life had gone to pieces so long ago that he had got used to being alone. The grounds for his divorce was the old story that they didn't get on in bed; that was what she alleged. It wasn't that he hadn't done his bit, because he used to rack his brains to keep her satisfied and he did wonders with his prick. The thing is his wife saw lots of films, and sex in fiction was infinite, with women in droves being screwed against walls and in public toilets and screaming like pigs at the slaughter as they reached orgasm, and gradually she had come to the conclusion that making love was something else, not that crap he offered her on their routine bed. Somewhere else, Margo, her face lit up by a black eye, was getting her cocaine-addicted husband's breakfast ready, while he bawled her out in a style he had been perfecting for the last three years. In another house and another room, Willem was at that moment asleep. He worked nights at a job which had nothing to do with his ambitions; he had got a degree, on the basis of parental sweat and his own, only to end up, freshly cultured, in the gutter of unemployment of his speciality. He was beautiful in a way which immediately raised twisted suspicions and envy, something which, along with his ordinary appearance and his rather churlish manner, lessened his chances of finding a job in an architect's studio. To cap it all, his girlfriend, who was a half-baked snob, had left him for a wanker who bought her roses and wrote poems for her, replacing in her fickle female heart – as pragmatic as it was romantic – Willem's amazing virility with a flamboyant civil servant's post in the Tax Office. All the same, he wasn't going to lose sleep over the girl's departure, as there was gutsy pride inside him, and his plans included moving up in society and getting hold of women with class. Not far away, Vivian and Patrick were arranging to meet as usual in the Byron. After getting drunk in the dive they'd take the car and hunt for a dark corner in some back street where they could get on with it on the seat. The receiver turned into an erect phallus for Vivian as she listened to Patrick eagerly telling her about a possible new place, pleasantly tucked away with views of woodland.

In the course of the day, an endless, devilishly hot summer day, Anita had become more and more despondent. The heat was softening her promises of purity. She missed those brutal caresses, she longed for the presence of some he-man who would dislocate her slight muscles and break her fragile bones in the lap of desire. She had had to put off her doubts about celibacy for urgent reasons of work. That night she had to work as well. She had a script to finish without delay so that she could hand it in next day, and she had to consult the station archives. In much the same way, Maurice the photographer had spent the day thinking about his reportage, interspersed with his insatiable ex-wife, and back to his reportage, obsessed: photographs of a building zat night to illustrate an interview whose content had irritated him no end. What threw him was why the magazine was interested in a nutcase like that, a guy who referred to himself as a "sexologist of matter" and who spent his time studying the erotic behaviour of different buildings, no less. Amongst the most absurd and overblown theories which had made him famous was the supposed homosexuality of the Chrysler Building in New York or the growing impotence of the Palace of the Alhambra in Granada. The stupid dick said that man puts his semen in everything he does and all his works could be analysed according to their erotic charge. Of this particular building he had to photograph, this foolish charlatan maintained that it was hermaphroditic, male and female in one, a fluid, living body, complete and of a piece, but riddled with easy to reach, welcoming orifices; female on its back, with a cunt lodged on the roof, wet and open, and male face down, its male member a beam anchored in the earth. The attraction of opposites, *yin* and *yang*, fuck. Then he described the inside of the building and claimed that the boardroom was a repressed prude who complained about the promiscuity in there, all because there was a couple who spent their lunch hours screwing on the table, when nobody was about; and he went on to say that the lift was gay and bent into the bargain, that the work areas were militant feminist lesbians, and what's more exhibitionists, because there were no dividing walls or doors, that the dining-room was a sadist who got it together with the cutlery, and another three pages of bullshit of this sort. Maurice had scornfully considered the idea of jerking himself off in the building to the health of this clown, this amateur who didn't even know what sex was. Sex had fucked his marriage up. In another street and another house, Margo was mechanically and silently detesting her decadent husband. That very night she had to do a special request. She led a secret life so as to make enough to get by on, because her husband, who was lavish only in matters of drugs, didn't even give her enough for a pair of knickers. The cynic said it turned him on for her to go without underwear. The fact is that she had finally got used to marital meanness and every time she secretly put on a pair of knickers or a bra she felt the same agreeable sensations as an adolescent smoking a forbidden cigarette, but also the same discomfort, strangeness and displeasure that the first fags produce in the would-be smoker. For Willem, though, it was just another ordinary common or garden night, with naps on the control panel, his cheddar sandwich and his architecture magazine, his time-worn mock-up filled with dreams, his list of jobs on offer from the paper, his eternal c.v.s and the complete syllabus of his first course in seduction for job interviews. And finally there he was, at the usual time, sitting with one eye on the closed-circuit television, watching the stars through the window, yawning, turning over pages and biting his bread.

At 21:52 a call comes on the doorphone.

Willem sees in the monitor that it's a woman. He asks her over the mike to identify herself and she says she works in the building and that she's come to consult the archives. She shows him her card and Willem checks it. Finally he lets her in. Anita is wearing a light, almost transparent linen suit, with thin straps and a plunging neckline, Willem can't help looking her over, from head to toe, and getting stuck on the neckline. Anita, who's feeling hot and absent-minded, neither notices nor processes the night watchman's ecstatic look: even so, an imperceptible smell, a certain bony width, a shining neck, a low-pitched voice, the all- pervading presence of the archetypal he-man, gradually percolates her as she makes her way to her desk.

At 22:14 a call comes on the doorphone.

Willem sees on the monitor that it's a man. He asks him over the mike what he wants and the caller says he's got permission to take photographs of the building by night. He holds up a piece of paper and the watchman lets him in. Now he remembers that the incident sheet mentioned a visit by a photographer. Maurice comes into the vestibule and starts wandering around. The building strikes him as strange: there are no offices or dividing walls, the desks, on which computers grow like mushrooms in season, are scattered around the different spaces formed by the design of the building in unequal groups, while various metallic or concrete elements grow out of the floors and walls: unexpected columns, staircases winding snakelike in a labyrinth of forms, glass galleries, walls that dissolve or shapes that surround and trap the visitor and won't let him go. Maurice looks round fascinated as he remembers the contents of the interview. He feels strange here. The fact is that he's never left his semen inscribed in any work – well, maybe in some of his photographs, but he's not sure. Perhaps because he's always been at war with his nether parts. Suddenly, out of the blue, he imagines the labourers on the scaffolding ejaculating into the concrete as they raise this building with their phallic trowel strokes, and then he fantasizes over a group of cleaning women rubbing themselves against that living body and masturbating it with their damp cloths. He takes more and more photographs, shooting frantically, as though hoping to kill this obscene sort of living being he's got into. Catching hold of a concrete hill that suddenly grows out of the floor and rises to meet the ceiling, he climbs up it with difficulty and gets into the little gap at the top of this sort of sucking tongue. And from this dark, damp cave that licks sweetly at his impotence, in a panoramic sweep of his zoom, suddenly through the window a parked car comes into view of his lens, and on the other side of the windscreen he clearly sees a young couple screwing completely naked with the front seats down. Fuck me, what a day, thinks Maurice. Everything reminds him of his failure, his incapacity, his ruin. The fact is that he can't take his eyes off the way those two arses are moving, and the rhythmic vibration of the car, and the four legs and four arms plus two torsos entwined in a randy tangle of sensuality. The guy must be a well-hung brute, to judge from the look on her face and the force with which he keeps shoving.

It's now 23:04.

Anita has sneaked into one of the soundproofed radio studios because the nightwatchman has filled her to the marrow with desire and she can't wait any longer. Here she thinks she'll be free from alien eyes and ears, and the golden padded walls of the cubicle seem to her like a sensual, all-surrounding beach in which she can indulge herself at will. She lifts her dress up, slides her lace knickers down a bit, puts her finger in and starts rubbing shamelessly as she thinks of that monster of nature in his uniform making her his with animal brutality. She forgets that Willem has been hired to watch every little nocturnal movement and that for that reason, and because this bird really turns him on, he's followed her there over the panel of monitors.

When he sees her in that state he gets an instant hard-on and decides that he too wants to masturbate imagining he's with her.

At 23:10 another call comes on the doorphone.

Willem, caught off guard, attends the new visitor as he pulls up his trouser zip without having finished the job. A woman wrapped in a gabardine is holding something in her hand. She says her friend Tony has sent her with an urgent delivery. Willem lets her in. She starts to unwrap the parcel and takes out a portable tape recorder which she then switches on. At the same time, Anita, who can find no peace, who is so filled with carnal desires that she can't keep a grip on herself, on life or on her work, walks towards the vestibule with an excuse ready so that she can see the watchman again at close quarters. Just by chance, Maurice is heading the same way because he needs to get into a room that's locked. The two meet downstairs at the exact moment when, with a shout of "Surprise!", an unknown woman is taking off her gabardine, as she sings "Happy Birthday" and dances suggestively to the sound of gentle, seductive music. The sight of her in her red underwear – garter, corset, tiny bra, minute tanga – has Willem rooted to the spot, with his mouth open and a noticeable bulge in his trousers. Anita and Maurice, motionless at the end of the staircase, gripping the handrail, watch in awe the movements of this unexpected star of the evening, who ends up completely naked on stiletto heels, swinging her hips, hugging herself, clawing at herself with long red nails and hanging her tongue out like a lizard on heat, all in time to the music. Maurice, as though waking from a dream, looks at the woman with unexpected tenderness while Willem tries unsuccessfully to put the gabardine over her. This is a woman who will do anything to seduce, who wants to be desired. Maurice knows all about that, he understands perfectly, and for that reason, and because he's always wanted to be a hero, he snatches the gabardine from the night watchman, pushes him to one side, puts his arm around the naked woman and starts to praise her performance in sweet, flattering tones, while she looks at him entranced, unable to believe what's happening. Anita, who's feeling terribly jealous, can't take her eyes off Willem's bulge; the excessive stress hasn't managed to bring it down to its normal size. The night watchman returns her look sadly, as if to tell her she needn't worry, that that's not his style, that he's hers and only hers, in spite of the show.

It's 23:45 and another call comes on the doorphone.

Willem consults the monitor again and sees a young couple locked together and looking distressed. They ask for help. The watchman, whose job is getting on top of him, lets them in without asking for any identification. When they finally reach the vestibule, the occupants watch them shuffle along locked tight together with their trousers undone. They explain, shamefaced and out of breath, that they were screwing in the car when her vagina suddenly contracted, trapping his penis tight inside her. They can't separate and it hurts a lot. The four spectators immediately start trying to help, and after a struggle in which they eventually get them both stripped off, the naked dancer, the horny watchman, the randy scriptwriter and the sentimental photographer discuss the best way and each of them grabs hold and starts pushing and pulling and shouting and gasping over the flesh of the poor victims, each one brandishing a different theory on how to get the two bodies apart.

In this state of affairs, at 00.32 another call comes on the doorphone. Willem, who's ready for anything now, lets go of his part of the prey, looks at the screen and recognizes the company director, who, it seems, is accompanied by a group of Asian top executives and their wives and who orders him to open the door for them. He uses an imperious tone of voice and seems browned off. He adds that there's a pair of dogs copulating in the bicycle park and says to come down at once to separate them and get rid of them, because they give a bad impression. The watchman's eyes fill with dread and, thinking as fast as he can, he decides to get everybody out of there on the double, and while he gathers together the clothes scattered over the floor – garter, corset, bra, jeans, T-shirts and gabardine – a group of people, three of them doing their best to drag a yoked couple along with them, get into the lift. An instant later, Willem rushes in behind them, after flipping the switch that opens the main door and abandoning his post, with a pile of clothes in his arms. The journey in the lift seems never-ending, the young couple have a fit of hysterics in their naked embrace, howling desperately, Maurice is pressed up against Margo's crutch and tits, and, not knowing what to do with his hands, he puts them behind the naked dancer, instinctively grasps her arse and just the upward movement and the general turmoil presses her body against his abdomen, instantly provoking an enormous and unheard of erection. Willem, with a tanga in his mouth and a pair of knickers hanging from his ear, tries to sort things out, at the same time as Anita, obstinately taking advantage of the fact that the watchman is almost buried under the gabardine and other clothes, pulls down his zip and grabs hold of his member, which is abidingly hard. And so they get to the top floor, the doors of the lift open and the lift dumps its human contents on to the roof terrace, freeing the couple of their pubic ties at a stroke.

It's exactly 00.39.

Margo and Maurice, Willem and Anita, and also Vivian and Patrick following suit, mate on the lawn on top of the building, in the heat of the summer, in time with the dogs in the bike park, by the light of the stars, but above all, before the stupefied gaze of a man frozen before the surveillance panel and surrounded by Asian visitors and wives who, silently diplomatic and imperturbable, huddled behind their host, watch the curious spectacle with apparent respect and reverence for foreign customs.

A touch of Ruysdael [1] in the air

Arjen Mulder

Nice North Atlantic light, right. And no rain at last.

That must be it.

Closed front.

I suppose it's the organization's critical attitude. Critical, somewhat leftist minds dislike openness. And because of the gay colors, they may be thick, but at least in a decorative way.

Er.

There - or...?

It's a stairway to heaven, like they had in those old television shows.

The quizmaster descends in a sparkling blue suit, waving his outspread arms; for a moment, there is the flash of a tooth in his enchanting smile, and his hair is shiny with brilliantine among the stars in the sky, which happens to be vibrating because they still needed these huge lights back then, so they had to cool everything down with...

No. It's a dike. On entering, you walk up onto the dike. Beyond it there must be a sea, an emptiness, a beckoning distance, a world of unlimited possibilities, *mare liberum*, freedom, openness, trading grounds - the sea is on the inside.

Out here, we are behind the dike, standing on drained land. A murmuring sea, that's right. Or a river. The elevation of the dikes has already turned out to be a success.

1 Salomon van Ruysdael (1603-1670), Dutch painter

Nice little beam.

At my grandfather's sawmill they distinguished between two kinds of trunks. They had to put those enormous things in the lake in front of the mill for weeks or months at a time before they could start sawing, or else the wood might get warped. There were all kinds - oak, pinewood, walnut, sycamore - and they all came in two varieties: floats and sinkers. Now these trunks were taken to the mill through the canals and ditches, sometimes straight from the spot where they had been cut down. They made rafts out of them, which they poled along with long sticks. One time, a mill hand on one of these rafts heard nature's call and shat over the side of the raft into the water.

So the mill hand on the other side of the raft shouted, 'What have you got, a float or a sinker?'

Nice anecdotes they are. You want a smoke?

No, what I mean is: whether it's a parody of that stairway to heaven or another version of the dike and the events at the sawmill, these youngsters are, as crazy and modern as it may appear, as Dutch as they come. Look at that table.

You blame me for the innocent look in my eyes.

Coffee, sirs?

Thank you.

Lately and now I suppose they expect us to blindly follow suit and this and that, and the whole diktat of topicality is an outmoded concept. If your medium has become outdated, why should you be any different.

Damned good cup of coffee.

I've forgotten how you like yours.

Two lumps of sugar, please. How about you?

Black.

You blame me for not using my brains.

I'm taking off. See you later, perhaps.

You blame me for not promoting you.

Need a discussion about what the hell we've been up to during the whole twentieth century. All that philosophical rubbish about the future of you digital smart-asses. That future will end in the year 2000, when all those machines will get jammed and we will not be able to get our money out of the bank for weeks or months on end and all the planes will be grounded and what do you mean, I'm being defeatist? I'm thinking forward, is what I am. Instead of your endless starting with the solution, we know all about that by now, thinking back from the end point.

Let me see if I can find a toilet.

You're leaving?

A stapler? I think there's one over here.

Have you got any staples too?

Not that I know of.

In that case, you can keep your stapler as well.

You blame me for not being such a responsible intellectual as you are.

Not in the mood today. A little too much grass over the weekend, I think.

In our studio today. World-famous in Germany and recently in America as well, but here, in their motherland, no one has ever heard of them. And sitting next to them there's our cultural philosopher.

You blame me for taking a historical approach instead of a topical one.

For twentieth-century folks, there was no more cheerful news than that man was a past station, that the last primitive societies had finally been exterminated, that even the remotest corners of the rain forest were now being cut down, that the ozone layer was dissolving over our very heads, that the chain reaction (DDT, PVC, CO_2) had set in irrevocably - no more cheerful productivity, more profound creativity, more sincere authenticity even, than through the awareness that we were the last ones, the end of all things. That was the myth that carried the twentieth century, that which gave us our awareness and rendered it bearable.

You blame me for not simply preferring motion to a standstill.

I'm too old for this stuff.

Fresh air, you mean. Meanwhile, the kids keep dropping over the edge.

Fuck this shit.

You blame me for believing that progress is taking place.

The further we are removed from the twentieth century, the more obvious it becomes that the era knew nothing but traitors. Those who did nothing should have gotten involved; the ones who did should have shut up. Refugees should have stayed put; the people who stayed at home should have scrammed. Artists should have explored the nature of technology;

technologists should have left art well alone.

Communists should have manipulated sexual desire; Fascists should have looked towards the other. Democrats should have woken up; the rich should have looked beyond their class interests.

You blame me for asking you whether *you* don't think you're telling the truth. What on earth did those twentieth-century folks *do* with all the energy and resources they wasted?

Time for a musical intermezzo.

The only way to render complexity endurable is to trust in it. Of course I don't know what will happen if you go around that corner, or climb into that pit, or cross that imaginary line - all of them singular points. All I know is that - just as intellectuals in the first half of the twentieth century were forced to acknowledge - the earth is round. It has no end. Everything goes on forever. That is the experience of the desert. All the efforts to survive in a barren environment, and then, after a while, the understanding of the futility of all human aspirations.

You blame me for not thinking that all of Derrida's disciples can go to hell.

Do not be ashamed of what you know, do not be proud of what you don't know.

Because they believed in surrender to the unknown, to the miraculous, to revelation, if you will. The recognition of the unrecognizable, the recognition that a thing may not be recognizable, and then to go for it all the way. To them, the world was not real in and of itself, it took effort, reality was a conscious act, a statement. Not a model, not a program, not a space of possibilities or technological potential, or an unexpected overlap between two systems, or some other sample of practical catastrophe theory. Life consisted of waiting, of attentively waiting, for something to approach. And when the event finally announced itself, no, if the sign which announced the event appeared, it was followed unconditionally.

You blame me for not having chosen a scientific career. You blame me for reading page-turners on the train. You blame me for not having attended your lecture. You blame me for speaking for the wrong radio stations. You blame me for still being in touch with them. You blame me for leaving instead of arguing. You blame me for having stayed with that company for far too long. You blame me for having read the latest Baudrillard. You blame me for not wearing modern glasses.

Thinking about the media has been *pataphysical* [2] from beginning to end, because it assumed that things were metaphysical, relationships, concrete. I am talking about information. Information as a thing does not exist. Information as a value, as a measurable quantity, does not exist. The nervous systems which supposedly receive and process information receive nothing from the outside, and transmit nothing to each other and the senses and muscles, that has not long since been stored in the structure of those very

2 The *pataphysics* were created by Alfred Jarry in 1898 as the science of imaginary solutions and the way to study the laws about exceptions. Among others (Queneau, Ionesco, Clair, Prévert, Robillot), Boris Vian was also member during the fifties of the Association of *Pataphysics*.

neurons etc. We receive no instructions from the outside. Information is not a thing, but a relationship; that is, the relationship between the known and the unknown. Information is an unlikely combination of elements. All that is not unlikely is uninformative. This means that information is the least significant ingredient of the news. You may safely go on a three-week holiday, no matter how great the assumed global crisis; on your return people will still be just as upset or unupset about the so-called crisis as when you left. News hardly changes, and should anything come up, it will be channeled in such a way as to render it likely, and therefore uninformative, non-news, again in no time.
Wait a second. Um.
Will take a few minutes.
Cup of tea, please.
I'll have a *Perrier*.
After this, can we continue our discussion about how to plan unexpected connections?
I thought I loved her.
Don't kid yourself - or her.
Do you know me?
You blame me for asking money for my work. You blame me for finding your TV show too stupid for words. You blame me for not keeping in touch after you had told me about the trouble you were having with your relationship. You blame me for not having turned up at the hospital to admire your baby. You blame me for not showing enough interest in your projects. You blame

me for not encouraging you to finally finish your book.

You blame me for not showing up for months because I had to finish mine.

You blame me for starting up my own bussiness.

Death is a porpoise washed up on a Dutch beach.

A caved-in sand dune.

For media really do not transmit information - or what exactly did you mean when you spoke of relationships - but they conjure up an entire environment, with its own sort of reality. Outside of it, the normal world is still visible, but it is only functional as a view, as the inessential that serves as a confirmation of the significance of everything that goes on in here. In here, there is a medially programmed reality that extends into all the remote corners of a space it has created itself. I mean: People understand each other because they share the same point of view, not because they have been convinced or persuaded to do so, or whatever.

The idea was already there, and then they recognize it - or think they recognize it - in somebody else's statement or proposal or plan, or building, right, and they eagerly jump at it. You only understand what you're saying to one another if you are in the same medial space. But if you understand the principle of various medial spaces, and if you can make a correct judgement as to what space your interlocutors are in, you can take them for a complete ride in terms of their medially induced premises. They will be happy to embrace your plans, and will fail to recognize that their own, well, let's say their own ideology is being used against them. They will go happily frolicking off into the hell of their own realized prejudices.

And what have you got to say?

Er. Thank you. Never again, and still not. Looking back on the twentieth century the conclusion forces itself upon us: No matter how much this century has managed to deny, it has never managed to live up to its promises, its happy certainties - the new man, the actually existing empire of freedom, self-determination, total transparence, virtuality. The genius of the century consisted of its capacity to demolish; in its domain architecture - any architecture - disappeared. Currently, humanity collectively inhabits the world instead of the town, nation, or continent; the infrastructure that will link anything to everything is *in statu nascendi* or has been realized for years - and still we die, all of us.

You blame me for having fallen in love with someone who does not belong to our circle. You blame me for not rejecting contemporary literature. You blame me for never going to squatters' bars any more. You blame me for having employed a housekeeper. You blame me for being a nonsmoker and a nondrinker.

If any solidarity has been created at all, it is physical: we are all stuck on the same little planet and keep each other informed as to how we're coping, or not, until the end. This is no place for us, and we know it. The next step? Where media deny corporality in order to increase speed, the next step can be no other than the disappearance of the bodies themselves.

Let us conclude with a literary contribution. We have invited three gentlemen who were going to explain the whole thing to us. So I thought, why not ask for a literary contribution - our esteemed theoreticians do not object to practical literature, I hope? - from the succesful one as well.

Jesus.

The writer was fond of coincidences which, provided you had the presence of mind, suggested a coherence of the world which at least philosophically speaking no longer existed. All those authors, those strange authors, who made up his canon had experienced something, something that had given them their specific view on things and people, something real, a terrible or wonderful incident, an insight for which faith is too weak a word. Their observations and language were a physical expression of this experience, which they never wrote about if they were any good; their style was embedded in their bodies, in their eyes and hands. For two or three hours a day he turned into one who toils alone, ten hours or more if a deadline had to be met; he would be completely out of it, detached from his social life, a tourist in the lonely experience of all those true masters of world literature. You just had to know how to organize it, give it a break for a few months every now and then. Do the complete young-writer thing; even Gertrude Stein would receive her friends from the art world before she sat herself down next to her oil lamp to write stack upon stack of paper, night after night. I'm addicted to writing, there is no other explanation. And so you, reader, can help me, for we all have our addictions. I offer you a touristic trip into mine. Once you close the book, the tour will be over. The most common cure against addiction is to have a baby; to have children is the most common excuse.

Which brings us to the end of.

Wasn't all that bad.

Don't kid yourselves. Nobody listens at this time of the day.

Except for those suffering from long-term unemployment. To which the intellectuals belong. I myself at least have enjoyed the state facilities to think things over in peace for eight years.

Alright, alright, we're leaving.

Where did the literary guy go?

Back to his safe solitude.

At the moment? Some translating, writing an article here or there. A lecture now and then. People love lectures nowadays. Live thinking, that's what they want to see.

Now that we're here. Where's the cafeteria? Nice shade of green.

You're going for the caterer's?

Still, all that bitching about the twentieth century is a form of hope as well, it's Utopian. That when all this crap will be said and done, we will witness something else, something better.

You got yourselves a nice theme with these media, I must say. Just take a look at what these youngsters do with their computers. I have no students left who do not produce a CD-ROM as their thesis. And why not. You have to innovate if you don't want to be left behind.

It's better to be left behind if the bus is headed for a cesspool.

Here, kind of macrobiotic, isn't it. Excuse me.

Upstairs, I guess. No, you can't go there.

Kind of nice.

Pretty open here at the backside. So critical people are closed in front, while at the back, they're caving in.

Or it is the escape clause offered to them to escape from their own self-righteousness. Get some fresh air every once in a while. Air the mind and all that.

Cheese sandwich. Ripe cheese. No, never mind the greens.

So you know your way around here?

Oh, yes, the philosopher with the Rotterdam accent. The one who's always going on about Bataille. I run into him every now and then at panel discussions.

A sandwich with chocolate sprinkles, if I can. And a glass of buttermilk. Because in this country architects make up the only profession that takes any interest in contemporary theory. All the others who are still trying to think under these sinking skies have become stuck with Heidegger or his postmodernist derivatives, to whom they object. Or vice versa.

Still, there's something we've failed to discuss. It may be said that a medium creates its own specific environment, but we forgot to mention that in that case, it is the task of theory to look for the gap in that environment.

Its antienvironment. Also, we haven't been very funny.

To look for an antienvironment is not the task of critical minds. Critics only serve to strengthen a developing environment by testing its strength, and by finding out where it needs further reinforcement. Just as hackers break right through security systems, not to prove that all that rhetoric about top security doesn't mean a thing, but in order to have computers even better secured. Hackers are critics.

And then the critics try their best to reanimate media that are as good as dead for a while. Not to abandon the old values before you've replaced them, that sort of thing.

You blame me for not wanting to be part of your informal network.

Outside on the lawn?

If the chocolate sprinkles do not get blown off of my sandwich.

You just need to press them firmly into the margarine.

Nice view of the treetops. Nice and quiet as well.

Critical, us? Not exactly.

Oh, yes, I remember those wonderful sentences: Whereas God needed two thousand years and humanity two centuries, it will take the media two decades at the most to disappear from the stage.

Yes, or how about: The media are already being exhibited in museums.

You blame me for putting aside less and less time for joint projects.

You mean the museum for new media in Karlsruhe? [3] Even before the turn of the century each and every medium has been saved from destruction, or,

3 ZKM, *Zentrum für Medientechnologie* or Centre for Media Technology, Karlsruhe.

rather, from the boredom which all that twentieth-century crap will be met with within ten or twenty years. Just as in that movie featuring Sylvester Stallone [4], in which he wakes up somewhere during the next century after having been frozen in ice, and all that people remember from our age are the silliest advertisement tunes. The rest has faded, crumbled, and has been forgotten.

You blame me for not having an opinion about the subjects of my writing. You blame me because I like to work.

It is rather the pleasure of maintaining an impossible position. Or of putting a lot of effort into a project that is doomed to fail. To become a striker in success, to refuse to present a theory that is of any use to people, or at least that will not gain anyone any power or high positions. To set sail on an expedition over the edge of the media planet, in the knowledge that it is round.

That we will always be tourists; that we are on a tour, going in circles, and will always return to the starting point.

Quiet. There.

Storks, I should think.

Infinity illuminates me. Infinity flows through my spinal cord.

I have loved you so much.

The principle is that, whereas inside, you never know exactly where you are

---

4 *Demolition Man* (1993) Director: M. Brambilla.

- or always have a place to go at least, are always someplace on a vector with no internal horizon to provide orientation -, up here on the roof you are suddenly provided with a natural horizon anc can leave the whole mess behind you.

You blame me for not acknowledging that you had grown up to become a mature woman.

The big mistake, I believe, of the twentieth century, of the twentieth-century avant-gardes, was that they believed that the old had to be completed or destroyed first before there would be room for the new to begin. The reason why the principle of criticism is now bankrupt is because ever since the '80s, especially since '89, it has become clear that the new is not a farewell to the old, but a recombination of older elements. That is the technological view of history. Technological minds are not interested in the ideologies with which they are confronted; ideologies belong to the materials from which they construct their systems, their devices, their links between bodies and machines. If an ideology still functions somewhere, use it, try to purify it, in order to realize the desires of the ideologues in that ideological space. Technology is not about efficiency, it is about passions.

You blame me for acting as if nothing had changed between us.

In a recombinant culture, the point is to create the unexpected connections, to plan the unforeseen. It has nothing to do with criticism, it has to do with creating informative situations, creating unlikely combinations. It is a most uncritical occupation: the point is not to find the right combinations, and therefore to reject others as wrong; it is to create as many combinations, as many connections as possible, along any possible route, any possible link. It doesn't matter whether you work with politically correct or incorrect ideas and attitudes, as long as you manage to create so many connections that in the end every ideology will evaporate, and all that remains is to enjoy the possibilities of the network. You give people what they want, you quote whoever you like, and in the end it turns out that desires change, the quotes subside from memory, the old gradually shifts into the new, and criticism is left out in the cold.

You set a fatal process in motion; where the ship will run aground is irrelevant.

Or the whale.

Yes.

Amen.

So that is the new religion?

It has nothing to do with *New Age*. *New Age* is critical. We want the *Next Age*. Always.

You blame me for not blaming you for anything.

There's an elevator over here.

What I mean to say is that the new, of which the twentieth century had so many dreams, and which it pursued so violently – that the new is not a thing, not a work of art, not a piece of architecture, no environmental design, but a relationship. The relationship between known elements, which is itself unknown however. The new is a combination.

You blame me for having given up on you just like that.

Are you still there?

Er. I think that in a world of some six thousand million people you can no longer demand or expect that people come up with original thoughts. Authenticity is possible as long as the world is not too crowded. But what you 'can' ask for, or strive towards, is, um - I mean, a thought is good if you have come up with it yourself. Even if it may turn out that several millions of people have had the same thought already. It doesn't matter. That is why I have nothing against tourism. The areas or cities or museums you visit have already been seen and visited by countless numbers of people, but now it's your turn. Now it's you who makes your own world out of them.

You're a romanticist.

I don't know the meaning of the word romanticism.

Let me put it this way: You're a sensitivist. You are only interested in your own impressions, your own experiences.

Which I will not have denied or prescribed to me by the media we are forced to use.

You blame me for not finding drugs mind-expanding.

Shall we go back? You want to walk?

You blame me for submitting obscure interviews. You blame me for being a lousy listener. You blame me for always talking too much. You blame me for not showing enough initiative.

Hey, it's him again.

Looking for a bite as well.

I don't think they're here.

The ceiling is just as low as in the attic where they sat before, though.

And the computers are still the same.

But look at all this stuff!

You blame me for just letting you die.

Judging from all the empty spots here, it seems they work with freelancers as well.

Wow, man, what is this. Huh? An amphitheater? Nice cabinets, with all those little holes.

I thought they had managed to design the building in such a way as to make it impossible to hang any paintings from the walls.

Come on, those Thirld-World paintings aren't that bad.

A combination of transparence and opacity.

Exactly. That is the point. You shouldn't combine things or ideas, that's something the users of your combination can supply themselves. People like to surround themselves with bric-a-brac. We feel most at home in a culture of trinkets.

Seventies tune?

That explains the rug and chandelier. You blame me for not being the father of your son.

I mean, you shouldn't combine signs. You have to combine combinations.

A network as a combination of networks, not of fixed points.

It is full of fixed points in here, but inasmuch as there are any signs, they have lost their original meaning by now, I suspect. They have become arbitrary remarks.

What you call information I call ludicrousness. The only really functional antienvironment is humor. Even art is institutionalized in no time. But a good joke will always be a good joke.

You blame me for never having undressed you.

This way. Now down. Let's hope your shoes don't slip.

Nice how it rattles underneath your wooden shoes.

A pleasant stay.

The only way to get rid of the twentieth century is if you can say, 'Oh well, it's only the twentieth century.'

Oh well, it's only a broadcasting network.

Oh well, it's only love.

Right, see you later.

Let me get a pack of cigarettes out of the machine.

Oh, hi there. See you later.

No, but if you want to ride along, go ahead. I feel more like walking around some more on my own.

To wait for the train.

We'll give us a ring then, next week or so.
Or send each other an e-mail.
They even have a little balcony up there.
Alone at last. Silence at last. Finally, finally. I have failed, but that is exactly my strength. I have not let that which was love slip back into mere fidelity. Or well, love, what do I know about it. It has not turned into folklore, the end of all culture. And you and I were a culture. As long as it lasted. I blame you for nothing, I'm sorry. You blame me for always saying 'me'. You blame me for not wanting to build a career. You blame me for still thinking about you, dreaming about you, my darling, my sweet darling.

the end

Publications about mvrdv and vpro

1994
De Architect (12)   December

1995
Nederlandse architectuur van de 20ste eeuw   August
Katalogus "Referentie: OMA", Nai Uitgevers

1997
De Architect   March
Archithese   3
Werk, Bauen+Wohnen (4)   April
Arch+ (136)   April
Architectuur&Bouwen   5
Archis   5
Algemeen Dagblad   1706
De Volkskrant   2706
De Gooi- en Eemlander   3006
Items (3)   June
Arquitectura viva (54)   May/June
Arquitectura VIA   0
Trouw   020797
Het Financieele Dagblad   05&0707
BouwWereld (13/14)   0707
Cobouw (128)   0807
NRC Handelsblad   0907
Het Parool   2908
Trouw   3008
Villa VPRO. De wording van een wondere
werkplek, VPRO   August
Domus (796)   September
De Groene Amsterdammer   1009
Archis (9)   September
TBI Bouwgroep   2109
Archithese (5)   September/October
AA files (34)   Autumn

Glas in Beeld (8)   October
Betonkrant, bijlage Cobouw (213)   1711
Cobouw (216)   2011
Bauwelt (43/44)   2111
Betonprijs 1997, Betonvereniging   November
Arquitectura Viva (57)   November/December
Items (7)   November
Bouw Elsevier (12)   December
NRC Handelsblad   3112
Architectuur&Bouwen (12)   December
Blueprint (145)   December
Frame (1)   December
Assemblage (34)   December

1998
El Croquis (86)   January
Neue Züricher Zeitung (21) Feuilleton   2701
Bouw Elsevier (1)   January
Berliner Zeitung (30) Feuilleton   0502
Zodiac (18)   September '97/February '98
Quaderns (219)   March '98
Elle decoration UK (68)   March
Metropolitan Home   March/April
El País   1804
Techniques & Architecture (437)   April
Jaarboek 1997/1998. Architectuur in Nederland, Nai Uitgevers
The Low Countries Arts and Society in Flanders and The Netherlands.
A Yearbook, Stichting Ons
Erfdeel
SI+A (6)   August
NRC Handelsblad   1509
A+U (336)   September
Archis   9
FARMAX. Excursions on Density, 010Publishers   October
Media and Architecture, VPRO / Berlage Institute   December

villa vpro

Headquarter and studios for the VPRO public
broadcasting company in Hilversum, 1993/97
Dudok Award 1997, Municipality of Hilversum
Concrete Award 1997, Betonvereniging

Client
VPRO Hilversum

Location
Mediapark, Sumatralaan 45, 1217 GP Hilversum,
The Netherlands

Project size
10.500 m²

Design
MVRDV: Winy Maas, Jacob van Rijs and Nathalie de Vries
with Stefan Witteman, Alex Brouwer, Joost Glissenaar,
Arjan Mulder, Eline Strijkers, Willem Timmer, Jaap van
Dijk, Fokke Moerel, Joost Kok

Facilitairy office
Bureau Bouwkunde, Rotterdam

Structure
Pieters Bouwtechniek, Haarlem and Ove Arup & Partners,
London

Services
Ketel R.I., Delft and Ove Arup & Partners, London

Building physics
DGMR, Arnhem

Acoustics
Centrum Bouwonderzoek TNO-TU, Eindhoven

Contractor
Voormolen Bouw BV, Rotterdam

Interior
Design of furniture items and interior consultancy
for the headquarter and studios of the VPRO
in Hilversum, 1996/97

Design
MVRDV: Winy Maas, Jacob van Rijs and Nathalie de Vries
with Joost Glissenaar, Eline Strijkers

Lighting
MVRDV with Robin Hood Produkties for a fluorescent
light fixture, 1996/1997

Sink
Peter Hopman

Pantry
Koot Productie (Jan Koot) and Peter Hopman

Signing
Fred Inklaar

Garden
Design for the communal garden around the head
quarters of Net 3 partners (VARA,NPS,VPRO,RVU)
in Hilversum, 1996

Design
MVRDV: Winy Maas, Jacob van Rijs and Nathalie de Vries
with Alex Brouwer in collaboration with Heidemij Advies

Client
NET 3, Hilversum

Contractor
Hogenbirk, Laren

mvrdv at vpro

Introduction
Jaime Salazar

PROJECT interface

Material supplied by
MVRDV Winy Maas, Jacob van Rijs and Nathalie de
Vries, Stefan Witteman, Nicole Meijer
VPRO Marjolijn Bronkhuyzen, Natalie Eckelkamp

The paradoxes were conceived by
Manuel Gausa and Jaime Salazar

Photographs
Louise Oeben (de "Niet in de Wieg gesmoord", pp. 40-41)
Hans Werlemann (pp. 28-33, 138-139, 142-143)
Coen Deckers (p. 83)
Hans Wilschut (pp. 133-135)

BUILDING interface

Photographs
Ramon Prat

FICTION interface

Stories by
Rafael Reig, F.M., Luís G. Martin,
Lola Beccaria and Arjen Mulder

Coordination
Editorial Lengua de Trapo
Javier Azpeitia, José Huerta

Photographs
Leendert Jansen
NOB Foto

Published by
ACTAR

Editor
Jaime Salazar

Graphic design
Ramon Prat

Translations
Peter Bijker
Andrew Langdon-Davies
Ozcariz-Lindstrom

Production
Font i Prat Ass.

Printing
Ingoprint SA

Distribution
ACTAR
Roca i Batlle 2 08023 Barcelona
Tel. +34. 93 418 77 59
Fax +34. 93 418 67 07
e-mail arquitec@actar.es
www.actar.es

DL B-22622/99
ISBN 84-89698-60-0
Printed and bound in the European Union